Walking with God

A Daily Devotional of Spiritual Truths in Poetic Form

Commander Michael H. Imhof, U.S. Navy (Ret.)

ISBN-13: 978-1-5725-8222-4 (Paperback)
ISBN-13: 978-1-4796-1406-6 (ePub)
Library of Congress Control Number: 2021906852

Cover format designed by Jodi Norrick
Special Thanks to A.F. Yarnell for administrative assistance and support

Published by

Table of Contents

Introduction

The purpose of this daily devotional is to convey truths of the Bible and how they apply to life in the area of successful everyday living. Using a unique way of conveyance, each date presents a daily message of spiritual truth in poetic form. The poetry is simple, but each poem has a clear message for all people in some way. I believe these poems have come from my heart with the help of the Holy Spirit. I believe you will gain something of value when you read each one of them. As you proceed through the calendar, I encourage you to ponder in your heart what is being said for each particular day.

In reality, each daily reading provides distinct and positive direction, much like a small sermon. I pray you will gain insight from each poem and apply it to your life as needed. I pray each one will encourage you. Value the truths of the Bible for the Bible is a special gift to man. It always leads us to victory because God is a good God and only wants the best for us.

It should also be noted that many of these poems can be easily integrated into sermon, or Sunday school material. For that matter, they can be used anywhere to magnify the Lord Jesus Christ in the lives of people. To God be all glory.

A DAILY DEVOTIONAL OF SPIRITUAL TRUTHS IN POETIC FORM

JANUARY 1

REBORN TO WIN

Adversity may come,
and adversity may go,
but there's one thing sure,
that I do know.

I'm going through.
I will survive,
and rise up,
for my spirit's alive.

No river is too wide,
that I can't cross.
No jungle is too thick,
where I'll become lost.

No mountain is too high,
that I can't climb.
Chains cannot hold me,
nor my hands bind.

Buildings may fall,
but I'll not shake,
nor will I crumble,
atop the earthquake.

The weather may blow,
with hurricane winds,
but I'll overcome,
for I'm reborn to win.

I'm going through.
I'm reborn to win,
for I'm now in Christ,
and redeemed from all sin.

Whatever the problem,
I'll overcome.
Whatever the circumstance,
I'll not succumb.

I'm reborn to win.
I'm now in Christ.
I have His righteousness,
and victorious life.

I'm redeemed from the curse.
No situation can defeat me.
I'm reborn to win,
and now have total victory.

JANUARY 2

RISE FROM THE DEAD

A man named Lazarus,
was raised from the dead.
Out of the tomb,
he was gently led.

Raised by Jesus,
Lazarus came forth,
to continue his walk,
and to finish his course.

Many years more,
Lazarus did live,
to share Christ with others,
and the gospel give.

He set up a church,
after Cyprus he went,
where he ministered the gospel,
and his years were spent.

You may have felt,
that you're at your wit's end,
with the rigors of life,
and its many bends.

If so, then look at Lazarus,
and what transpired.
Let it rejuvenate you,
and to you inspire.

Lazarus was a dead man,
but to life he came,
to serve the Master,
with more years gained.

You're not a dead man,
but still have breath,
so get on with life,
and your many years left.

Lazarus came back,
and encourages us,
to take off the linen,
and wipe off the dust.

Rise from the dead,
and pick up your life,
further God's kingdom,
and move forward in Christ.

JANUARY 3

HEAVEN

A place so beautiful,
words can not describe,
things prepared for you,
on the other side.

You'll see it in time.
It's just a small wait,
when your eyes will behold,
Heaven's pearly gates.

Joy will fill your heart,
when you first arrive.
You'll realize you're there,
this wasn't a lie.

You're an adopted son,
so shout for glee.
There's Lord Jesus,
waiting to meet thee.

Things of earth,
will grow strangely dim,
surrounded by love,
you'll focus on Him.

Forever you'll live,
in a place prepared for thee.
Acceptance of Jesus,
was the key.

No more cares or sorrows,
they've been washed away.
Oh! don't miss it,
it'll be a glorious day.

JANUARY 4

NOT A PACK RAT

Before you were born,
God already knew,
what He had planned,
specifically for you.

As He helps you along,
know for sure,
that His love hasn't waned,
but it will endure.

He's working in your life,
and putting things in your heart.
He's developing you,
as you do your part.

Set your mind on Him,
along with your affection.
He'll work in your life,
and bring proper direction.

As He works in your heart,
be assured of this fact.
God is not storing junk,
for He's not a pack rat.

As He stores nuggets,
they'll be nuggets of use.
God stores real well,
and will not abuse.

He knows what He's doing,
as He develops you.
Just trust in Him,
make sure you do.

Faithful is He,
as He stores each shelf.
Faithful is He,
with what He left.

God is a wise investor.
He knows what you'll need.
He's building you up,
to accomplish great deeds.

God is not a pack rat.
I say it again.
Bear with Him,
and you'll see His plan.

JANUARY 5

WEEKEND PRIORITIES

It's time for the weekend,
the boat's in the driveway.
Let's get on the road,
and go to the bay.

The greens are fine,
and so are the fairways.
It's a great day for golf,
it's a beautiful day.

Surf is up,
on the beach this day.
Let's get on down,
no more to say.

Turn on the game,
for it's Sunday.
Looks like a score,
get out of my way.

Time for Jesus,
well, He's ok,
but I'm too busy,
no more to say.

Go to church,
sometime I may,
but my priorities,
say not today.

JANUARY 6

ARE YOU KNOWN IN HELL?

The seven sons of Sceva,
were not known in Hell.
It's an interesting story,
that I will now tell.

To cast out a demon,
they used Jesus' name,
but the man responded,
by beating them to shame.

The evil spirit said he knew,
both Jesus and Paul,
but he didn't know them,
that paid this call.

Things from the Holy Spirit,
must be received in revelation.
The seven sons of Sceva,
had not received salvation.

Man must open his heart,
and come to the Lord.
Revelation will then grow,
as he stays in the Word.

Jesus defeated Satan,
many years ago.
Those in Christ,
are to show he's a defeated foe.

Lack of knowledge,
have kept many Christians down,
but I'm here to remind them,
that in Christ they're on solid ground.

A man in Christ,
if he'll receive this instruction,
is called to destroy,
Satan's works of destruction.

What I say,
is not subject to opinion,
for one in Christ,
is called to execute dominion.

Come against Satan's works,
and this I'll tell,
that as you demonstrate his defeat,
you'll be known in Hell.

JANUARY 7

SON OF PHARAOH'S DAUGHTER

Picture the fame,
Moses could have had.
To many Egyptians,
his decision was sad.

The son of Pharaoh's daughter,
he refused to be called.
He gave up his rich life,
to follow God's call.

Moses had to decide,
if he was going to live for self.
He gave up benefits, rights and privileges,
and from Egypt he left.

The dilemma of Moses,
is common to man,
to live for self,
or to follow God's hand.

Moses wanted God's will.
It was a decision made.
Plans of the exodus,
would soon be laid.

A quality decision,
Moses did make.
His trust in God,
one could not shake.

On this point,
let's shift our gears,
and ask of you,
about your years.

Are you living for self,
or following God's plan?
This question is common,
to all of man.

JANUARY 8

GO TO THE ROOTS

Stop the flow of drugs,
it's ruining our society.
Just say, "No!",
so much better it'll be.

Let's have gun control,
keep them out of peoples' hands.
Stop the crime,
it'll be a better land.

More rapes have occurred,
they're on the increase.
Lock the criminals up,
then we'll have a decrease.

Teenage pregnancies bother you,
they're high you know.
Educate on condom use,
then they'll be low.

The tree has many branches,
limb by limb you'll see,
however, look deeper,
before you reply to me.

Go to the roots,
it's there the problems lie.
It's spiritual,
for the old self must die.

Old things will pass away,
when a nation has spiritual revival,
and if men will listen closely from their hearts,
they'll truly hear God's call.

People need Jesus,
the answer to life's needs.
People must be reborn,
then you'll see better deeds.

JANUARY 9

TRUST IN HIM

A presence I can not see,
at least with my physical eyes,
yet, I know He's there,
I won't believe the devil's lies.

Jesus died for me,
the Bible tells me so,
on Calvary's tree,
many years ago.

His blood speaks loud,
it continues to shout,
of Christ's great victory,
there's no doubt.

He's my Savior,
of this I know,
for I accepted Him as Lord,
many years ago.

I've been healed,
and my life restored.
It's easy for me,
to call Jesus, Lord.

He speaks to me,
in that still small voice.
It's my Master,
in Him I rejoice.

A fellowship we have,
it's so sweet.
There's a wonderful joy,
it can't be beat.

He answers prayers,
and meets my needs.
He has never let me down,
please take heed.

I know that I know,
that He is true.
Experience has shown me,
in all that I do.

Many things will pass,
but this I'm sure,
His Word will stand forever,
it will endure.

JANUARY 10

PROPHECIES

Only one holy book uses prophecies,
reasoning does tell,
that the others do not,
for they're inspired from Hell.

The devil can not match,
the Alpha and Omega,
for he'd make a mistake,
but not great Jehovah.

The Bible has stood the test of time.
Throughout all the ages,
history and archaeological evidence,
corroborate the wise sages.

Prophets spoke forth,
inspired by the Holy Spirit,
words with future meaning,
pondering all of it.

Throughout history,
man has recorded many events.
Yes, he has recorded history,
but God writes it.

Pie in the sky,
some may say,
but history says different,
to this very day.

Prophecies have been fulfilled,
with amazing accuracy.
Open your eyes,
and then you'll see.

The Bible is real,
spoken from the Father's heart,
each and every word,
each and every part.

JANUARY 11

GOD IS ON YOUR SIDE

God is a good god,
only believe.
He'll never let you down,
don't be deceived.

He wants to bless you,
in abundant ways,
and surround you with His love,
throughout all your days.

Blessings are yours,
open your heart,
and receive from the Father,
He'll do His part.

El Shaddai is He,
it's one of His names.
He's more than enough,
this isn't a game.

His eyes are on the righteous,
He's open to their cry,
although the devil says differently,
don't believe his lies.

Cast your cares on Him,
He'll carry the weight,
and answer your prayers,
and won't be late.

Look to Him,
His hand is there.
Receive his love,
He wants to share.

Whatever you need,
He'll provide.
Always remember,
He's on your side.

JANUARY 12

SPEAK TO THE MOUNTAIN

The fig tree withered,
as Jesus spoke its way,
to bear no more fruit,
from that very day.

Jesus gave a lesson,
to his disciples that day.
Speak to the mountain,
and you'll have what you say.

Believe in your heart,
and speak words of faith,
for it's very important,
what you say.

Words do matter,
in our daily walk.
Watch your lips,
watch your talk.

Be strong in the Lord,
and make a good confession.
Being steadfast in Him,
will bring possession.

Victory is ahead,
you've set your course.
Don't turn back,
there'll be no remorse.

Stay on course,
His promises are true,
continue to thank Him,
as one should do.

Your answer will come,
there is a date.
Trust in Him,
it won't be late.

JANUARY 13

ANGELS

Mighty in stature,
they do stand,
to serve God and his servants,
each to a man.

Not to be seen,
with the physical eyes,
but they're there,
this isn't a lie.

Guardians of good,
from the Most High,
ministering to saints,
they stand nearby.

Promises of God,
they are enforced,
as people pray forth,
and set their course.

Hearken they do,
to the Word of God.
Always remember,
they're on your side.

They're there to help,
don't be deceived,
of their ministry,
do receive.

JANUARY 14

THE COMFORTER

The Comforter was sent,
from Heaven to Earth,
to reside in men,
who've received the new birth.

A promise was made,
before the crucifixion,
that He would be sent,
after the resurrection.

True to His word,
that Jesus made clear,
the Holy Spirit came,
a gift so dear.

To help believers,
in their daily walks,
know this is true,
this isn't just talk.

A gentleman He is,
to lead and guide,
from a still small voice,
with you He'll abide.

The wisdom of God,
comes forth from Him,
of great value,
worth more than gems.

In all situations,
open your sight,
and choose the best paths,
as you receive His light.

He's wants the best for you,
for He's so good.
Make no mistake,
this must be understood.

He'll never lead you astray,
on Him you can trust.
Walk with Him,
it's a must.

The Comforter came,
because of God's great love,
sent as a gift to mankind,
from Heaven above.

JANUARY 15

SATAN'S DEFEAT

Defeated he is,
that devil of old,
defeated by Jesus,
you may have been told.

Blood was shed at Calvary,
on a Jerusalem hill.
The devil moved in,
going for the kill.

He had Jesus,
so he thought,
dead at last,
it's what he sought.

There's more to hear,
lend your ear my way,
and listen very carefully,
to what I say.

Jesus died,
to be sure,
but the story continues on,
it does endure.

Keys from the devil,
to Hell and the grave,
Jesus forcefully took,
so mankind could be saved.

Principalities He spoiled,
a victory so complete,
forever the blood,
has sealed Satan's defeat.

Captivity set free,
because of God's masterful plan,
wake up and realize,
what God did for man.

JANUARY 16

AMBASSADOR

Christians represent the Lord,
don't you know it's true,
that they should be proper,
in everything they do.

Citizens of this land,
became enrolled in God's book,
when they accepted Jesus as Lord,
that's all it took.

They now represent,
the King of Kings.
Ponder these things,
and realize what this means.

The gospel must be shared,
to all that will hear,
to those afar,
to those that are near.

Be ever watchful,
for others to assist,
encourage them to receive Jesus,
and make Heaven's list.

Each has a calling,
no matter where one is placed.
Shine forth His light,
for others to receive grace.

Priorities have changed,
received from above.
You're now a vessel,
to show God's love.

Represent Him well,
you're now on assignment.
It's a daily walk,
and takes commitment.

JANUARY 17

GRAND REUNION

Grief shadows death,
at sometime in our lives.
It's part of living,
I do surmise.

Attachments are formed,
and do grow strong,
but too much grief,
can be wrong.

Lives will pass,
on this depend,
but realize this,
it's not the end.

All will live on,
after leaving here,
know for sure,
and hold this dear.

Those in Christ,
have a rich reward,
they've accepted Jesus,
and made Him their Lord.

To be absent from the body,
is to be with the Most High.
Put on a smile,
and replace that sigh.

Hard it may be,
as we grieve,
but eternal life,
they've received.

They're in a greater place,
and we've been left,
so get eyes on this,
and off of self.

Someday you'll see,
their smiles again,
waiting for you,
they have been.

A grand reunion,
it will be,
when we're all in Heaven,
just wait and see.

So keep your heads up,
and live for Him,
and realize in time,
you'll see all of them.

Change that frown,
and put joy on your face.
A celebration is coming,
so live in His grace.

JANUARY 18

FORGET THE PAST

Skeletons of guilt,
linger in the memories of our minds,
failures from past years,
that refuse to stay behind.

Thoughts are formed,
that pierce our hearts,
throbbings of pain,
that won't depart.

A cure is sought,
from this mental torment,
which way to turn,
looking for a hint.

Turn to Jesus,
He will forgive,
and take away your guilt,
and help you to live.

Sin He forgives,
this is so,
but He does much more,
you should know.

Strength comes forth,
when you accept Him,
and allow Him to live,
deep within.

Help is there,
as you look above.
Receive His peace,
accept His love.

Move forward with Christ,
the Bible does say,
and know He's with you,
throughout each day.

Forget your past,
it's dead and gone.
Receive in your heart,
a brand new song.

A bright future you have,
the past is dead,
so put up your chin,
and look ahead.

JANUARY 19

FORGIVE

It's so easy,
to hold a grudge,
to be so bitter,
and refuse to budge.

People do things,
that they should not,
creating ill will,
making tempers hot.

Unforgiveness is carried,
it's easy to do,
but people must guard against it,
no matter who.

Give it up,
for it is sin,
and hurts you more,
as it eats within.

Let it go,
and be set free,
walking in love,
is your key.

Remember the Lord Jesus,
and what He did for you,
forgiving your sins,
you should too.

JANUARY 20

CHRISTIAN PRIDE

People tend gardens,
keeping out the weeds.
A lesson can be learned here,
as we pursue good deeds.

Teaching Sunday school,
is good indeed,
working with children,
and planting good seed.

Leading the songs,
lifts up praise,
promoting the service,
in special ways.

Ushers do assist,
this is true,
helping many people,
in all they do.

Deacons are important,
supporting their pastors,
certainly this is pleasing,
to our Lord and Master.

Passing out tracts,
tells of salvation,
as many unsaved,
receive revelation.

The message is this,
it's quite clear,
guard your spirit,
and hold it dear.

Walk in humility,
and in it not doubt.
Serve the Lord with honor,
and keep pride out.

Our example is the Lord,
of good things He talked,
and through daily living,
in humility He walked.

We're all called of God,
and have designated roles.
We're to work where placed,
and help save men's souls.

JANUARY 21

KEEP YOUR CANDLE LIT

Remember the zeal,
that you first had.
You've now let it slip,
and this is sad.

On fire you were,
when you were first saved,
with great joy,
you did behave.

Your light was strong,
as you believed in Him,
but the flicker has diminished,
and has grown more dim.

Draw near to Jesus,
and he will draw near to you.
It's an important step,
a significant clue.

Never did He leave,
He's been there all along,
and wants to help you,
to put joy back in your song.

Get in His Word,
it will encourage you,
and think of His presence,
in all that you do.

Sing songs of praise,
another good start,
He'll inhabit your praises,
and renew your heart,

Get good teaching,
is another part,
attending the right church,
will encourage your heart.

Don't forget prayer,
the Lord does hear,
He knows all about you,
and holds you so dear.

Keep your eyes on Jesus,
He'll never let you down.
Remember someday,
He'll have you a crown.

JANUARY 22

BE NOT CONFORMED

Be like the crowd,
yes, be like the rest.
That's what the world says,
to pass its test.

Follow the rules,
and you'll blend in.
Don't upset the cart,
even if its sin.

The wisdom of this world,
is not from the Bible,
and if you follow it,
you're not a good disciple.

A few words I have,
keep them in your sight.
Stay with God's ways,
and do what's right.

You're in this world,
but not of it.
Keep this in mind,
and watch what you covet.

Man's attention,
it will surely pass,
but God's attention,
it will surely last.

So if you feel,
like you're a minority,
remember with God,
that you're a majority.

Be not conformed,
to the world's ways,
but stand for God,
throughout all your days.

A confidence will grow,
as you live right.
Others will notice,
as you spread God's light.

Be strong for Him,
a good witness be,
and you'll affect others,
just wait and see.

JANUARY 23

SMELL THE ROSES

Smell the roses,
a phrase we've heard,
one with meaning,
it has good word.

Cares of this world,
will rob you of peace.
They'll always be there,
and will not cease.

One must realize this,
on life's road,
and determine to do something,
about these loads.

Cast your cares on the Lord,
the Bible does say.
Give them to Him,
each and every day.

Then rest in peace,
and leave them with Him.
He'll carry each care,
all of them.

Your needs will be met,
from His mighty hand,
for He has them now,
in Heaven's land.

God wants you to enjoy life,
on earth's sod,
and know He'll provide for you,
a mighty God.

So let worry go,
and do not fret.
Keep your eyes on Him,
and you'll be set.

JANUARY 24

NOT A BABY, OR ON A CROSS

People buy pictures of Jesus,
and mount them on walls.
You can buy pictures of Jesus,
at Christian bookstores or malls.

He'll be pictured on the cross,
or in a manger with hay,
but more must be considered,
in light of Resurrection Day.

So many people,
when they think of Christ,
remember Him on the cross,
or as a baby in life.

Jesus is a resurrected Christ,
He's now off the cross.
He accomplished great things,
and gave victory to the lost.

Jesus is alive,
and intercedes on your behalf.
This should bring a smile,
or even make you laugh.

His resurrection power,
displayed at Calvary,
should be working in your life,
because He set you free.

Ask the Holy Spirit,
and He'll help you learn.
He'll reveal more of Jesus,
if you'll discern.

Jesus meets all your needs,
and helps you overcome.
Know His resurrection power,
and of defeat you'll not succumb.

JANUARY 25

INDICATORS

Don't pass judgment,
is good advice,
walking that way,
will not suffice.

Walking in love,
is a better way,
but please do listen,
to what I say.

Use your head,
in the affairs of life,
even when people,
are not so nice.

Watch their actions,
and you will tell,
those in danger,
of going to Hell.

People will say,
they believe in God,
but their actions betray them,
as they nod.

The devil believes in God,
oh, so well,
but his future isn't bright,
he's going to Hell.

People will cuss,
as they talk,
cussing the Lord,
as they walk.

Indicators are there,
let's perceive,
those that need salvation,
don't be deceived.

A relationship with Jesus,
is the key,
open their eyes,
so they may see.

Use wisdom,
as you watch them behave,
be led of the Holy Spirit,
and get them saved.

JANUARY 26

LIFEGUARD

Lifeguards are common,
around the water's edge,
to protect swimmers,
a safety hedge.

Presence is there,
for protection they seek,
of distressed swimmers,
in waters too deep.

Eyes are sharp,
as they scan the beach,
doing their duty,
with every peek.

The term lifeguard,
is an interesting name,
relating it to the cross,
wouldn't be in vain.

Life is forever,
in this one or next,
the Bible's my reference,
it's clear in text.

Protect your life,
look to the cross,
where Jesus died for you,
and all the lost.

The Word is on duty,
His love endures,
to grant eternal life,
it can be yours.

Look to the Lifeguard,
to save your soul.
Accept His shed blood,
as you've been told.

JANUARY 27

CHECK THE TIME

The clock is ticking,
watch its hands.
It's close to midnight,
watch God's plans.

The fig tree is budding,
the Middle East shows.
There's coming a time,
when Christians will go.

Man does not know,
the exact date,
but the Father knows,
it won't be late.

Be on guard,
and do His work.
Hold fast to your walk,
and do not shirk.

He's coming soon,
it's in the air.
Do not miss Him,
please don't dare.

Memories of Noah,
come to mind,
when so many,
were left behind.

It's the Blessed Hope,
of which I speak.
Get your house in order,
make sure it's neat.

Pay close attention,
to what I say,
for joy will fill,
the sky that day.

JANUARY 28

REPUTATION

It speaks loudly,
often out of sight,
of the man it represents,
during day or night.

How he lives,
has a keen affect.
Then couple with words spoken,
and direction is set.

Was he honest,
and kept his word?
Was he truthful,
in what was heard?

Did he care,
and reach out?
Was he unselfish,
is there doubt?

Hard working and diligent,
do speak well.
People take notice,
and thoughts will dwell.

Actions speak clearly,
was kindness seen,
or just the opposite,
was he mean?

Manners are appreciated,
and are observed,
so is rudeness,
if it's heard.

Reputation is made,
during the affairs of man,
reflecting his image,
to all the land.

JANUARY 29

PRAY IN FAITH

How to receive,
people do ask,
to receive more faith,
and make it last.

Use of time,
and how it's spent,
makes a difference,
here's the hint.

Listen to the Word,
and feed your heart.
Faith comes by hearing,
as seeds do their part.

Get right teaching,
and read your Bible.
Faith will stir,
for you're a disciple.

Water the seeds,
and as you sow,
they'll take root,
and begin to grow.

Let your words,
reflect your walk.
Make them faith-filled,
in all your talk.

Receive His promises,
and take a stand.
Trust in Him,
you surely can.

Keep watering your heart,
and guard against weeds.
Resist doubt and fear,
do take heed.

You have it now,
in the spirit realm.
The manifestation is coming,
trust in Him.

The answer will show,
on a certain day.
He'll be faithful,
in faith you prayed.

JANUARY 30

LIGHT DISPELS DARKNESS

A room may be dark,
when you walk into it,
but light a match,
and you'll see a switch,

Darkness may resist,
throughout the room,
but around the match,
light will loom.

Reasons exist,
why this is so,
for where light is,
there is glow.

Light dispels darkness,
a physical force.
It's the same spiritually,
and shines the dark course.

Lives will be saved,
as the gospel is shared.
Lives will be changed,
because someone cared.

Shine your light,
wherever you go.
Never keep it hidden,
always let it show.

It has an affect,
against Satan's domain.
People will be helped,
and be glad you came.

If the match is not lit,
the room will stay dark,
so begin to help others,
get on the mark.

Share with others,
and do exhort,
helping them obtain,
a good report.

The truth shines forth,
for people to see.
They're no longer in darkness,
but now set free.

JANUARY 31

WEDDING SUPPER

A bride prepares,
before the date,
wanting things in order,
for her mate.

Smooth the details,
let's make haste,
ensuring things are perfect,
and in place.

Fuss is made,
in all orchestrations,
a wedding is coming,
finish all preparations.

An invitation has been issued,
it's easy to receive.
Just accept Jesus as Lord,
and only believe.

A wedding supper it's called,
in Heaven you'll see,
where all saints will gather,
and forever will be.

Glorious in nature,
will be this event.
Glory to the Lamb,
the One who was sent.

It's easy to be there,
and to be a part.
Just ask the Lord Jesus,
into your heart.

A celebration is scheduled,
that will be great.
An invitation has been issued,
there is a date.

Don't think too hard,
nor hesitate,
for when the door closes,
it will be too late.

Oh, don't miss it,
it will be so grand.
Come to the Lord Jesus,
it's part of His plan.

FEBRUARY 1

DON'T PICK UP THE PACKAGE

Pick up the package,
and put it on your back.
Many people practice it,
and make it a knack.

Sometimes it's heavy,
and neatly wrapped,
drawing one's energies,
it will sap.

Worry is in order,
it comes with the deal.
It has been signed for,
it has your seal.

Talk about your troubles,
words you've rehearsed.
The package seems heavier,
it only gets worse.

Recheck the label,
and from whom it was sent.
You'll quickly realize,
it came with ill intent.

Resist the devil,
and give the package back.
Tell him to take it,
and put it in his sack.

You'll not sign for it,
for you have a better report.
You're a child of God,
and you have His support.

Cast the care on Jesus,
for His yoke is light.
Always remember,
He has you in sight.

He'll pick you up,
and see you through.
Keep your eyes on Him,
in all you say and do.

Your life will change,
if this lesson you'll learn,
realize you have the victory,
it's of Jesus' concern.

FEBRUARY 2

PRISM OF HOLY SPIRIT

A prism shines forth,
different shades of light,
creating a beautiful picture,
it's a lovely sight.

Several colors are there,
with different shades,
from the same source,
each was made.

Different fruits and gifts,
are referred to in the Word,
given from the Holy Spirit,
you may have heard.

Each one is wonderful,
in its own way,
helping the body of Christ,
from day to day.

Different colors contribute,
to nature's scheme,
so it is with the fruits and gifts,
there's a similar theme.

From the Holy Spirit,
these things are given,
to help the body,
obtain better living.

To move forward in Christ,
each has a role,
to help the body,
they're good for the whole.

When you look through a prism,
remember the comparison you've heard.
Think of the different fruits and gifts,
they're listed in God's wonderful Word.

FEBRUARY 3

DOER OF WORD

Being reborn,
covers the spirit part of you,
but it doesn't renew the mind,
that's for you to do.

Man's spirit,
wrestles with his flesh.
His thinking must change,
for them to mesh.

Walking in the world,
has had its affect.
One's thinking must change,
one must not neglect.

Study the Bible,
and learn God's ways.
Pay close attention,
and learn what it says.

As knowledge comes,
changes will be seen,
but there's something else,
that must be deemed.

Knowledge is great,
but a doer must be,
for one to walk,
in greater victory.

God's Word applied,
will help one grow,
and develop maturity,
you should know.

Obedience to the Word,
will bring great success,
in your Christian walk,
God does attest.

FEBRUARY 4

JESUS WILL NEVER QUIT ON YOU

As a Christian goes through life,
people may let him down.
People may quit on him,
and bring him frowns.

Human nature does this,
but I've got good news.
Jesus will never quit on you,
win or lose.

You may occasionally slip,
as on ice,
but He'll help you up,
and through any vice.

Come what will,
come what may,
He'll always be with you,
even during life's frays.

There will be times,
when the wind will blow,
but He'll stay there with you,
wherever you go.

No situation can come,
not one of them,
that can drive Him away,
as you remain in Him.

He's working things out,
to will and to do.
Be assured He's there,
to guide and help you.

Jesus will never quit on you.
I say this again.
Jesus will never quit on you,
for you belong to Him.

FEBRUARY 5

TORTOISE AND HARE

The race was set,
all gathered to observe.
The hare spoke loudly,
showing a lot of nerve.

The hare started quickly,
the start did sound,
gaining much distance,
covering much ground.

Victory seemed easy,
the tortoise was slow,
not much more distance,
not much more to go.

So the hare took a nap,
for his own sake,
giving the tortoise,
his big break.

The tortoise crossed the line,
while the hare did snooze,
allowing the tortoise to win,
and the hare to lose.

So here's the moral,
of this race,
don't quit running,
and avoid disgrace.

There's work to be done,
to be a fact.
You won't find shortage,
or a lack.

Run for Jesus,
find a good pace.
Endure and be strong,
and run a good race.

Well done you will hear,
on that day,
when the Lord speaks to you,
words of praise.

Pleasure you'll receive,
as rewards are given.
It'll be a joyous day,
for you in Heaven.

FEBRUARY 6

PETER CRIED WOLF

Peter cried wolf,
and fooled the town.
They came running,
at his sound.

Peter cried again,
three times it came.
The town came running,
results the same.

The wolf did come,
on one day,
but no answer from town,
to Peter's dismay.

Many people think,
that they can wait,
put things off,
and hesitate.

Salvation is now,
while one may choose.
Take too many chances,
and one may lose.

The wolf will come,
on one day,
and it'll be bleak,
for those not saved.

No one can help,
before they tried,
but now too late,
you've done and died.

Separated from God,
forever to be,
no more chances,
will one see.

FEBRUARY 7

TRIM YOUR WICK

The hurricane is coming,
people please hear,
all the signs are there,
it's coming near.

The volcano is set,
it's ready to go,
please take heed,
you should know.

People get ready,
and do prepare,
when nature calls,
with a scare.

The signs are there,
of the Lord's return.
Look to your spirit,
and do discern.

Fill your vessel,
quick with oil.
Remain planted,
and remain loyal.

Trim your wick,
the whole part.
Look to God's Word,
and guard your heart.

Know for sure,
it's coming near.
The signs are there,
please do hear.

Make your roots strong,
and grow them deep,
as you get ready,
for your Lord to meet.

FEBRUARY 8

AN ATHLETIC APPROACH

Athletes train hard,
during the day.
Listen more closely,
to what I say.

Discipline is seen,
as hours are spent.
Is there not a cause,
to be so diligent?

Preparation is in order,
it is the key,
striving to obtain,
complete victory.

As in the physical,
there's a spiritual theme.
To gain improvement,
use a similar scheme.

Spend time with the Lord,
and read His Word.
Meditate on the truth,
and what you've heard.

Worshiping together,
and gathering in His Name,
will help one's walk,
and fan the flame.

Effort is required,
to develop one's walk.
Actions are important,
and not just talk.

Push forward in God,
and be disciplined.
Then you'll gain victory,
in the end.

FEBRUARY 9

ANCHOR IN THE STORM

The boat drifts,
here and there,
when without anchor,
if you dare.

Anchors are made,
to hold boats in place,
guarding against drifting,
in every case.

In an unstable world,
truths must be learned,
embedded in your heart,
promises made firm.

Know who you are,
and what belongs to you,
as a child of God,
know what is true.

When the wind blows,
and storms do rise,
remain in place,
and do be wise.

Stand on the Word.
Be strong in Him,
and you'll beat the storms,
all of them.

Your anchor is strong.
It's based on the Word,
firm in your heart,
promises you've heard.

Don't drift away.
It does behoove,
to remain in the Word,
and all its truths.

FEBRUARY 10

A PRAYER FOR ALL

Petition the Lord,
for these things,
and most assuredly,
you'll not be the same.

That He would reveal,
the hope of His calling,
opening the eyes,
of your understanding.

An inheritance is yours,
purchased at Calvary.
Seek to know all of it,
for total victory.

Power is available,
for those that ask,
to accomplish mighty works,
eternity to last.

That you would be strengthened,
with His power,
through His Spirit,
this very hour.

To know the love of Christ,
that surpasses knowledge,
to grasp its breath, width, depth and height,
it takes more than college.

These things do cherish,
they're of the spiritual realm.
They're of great value,
each and every one of them.

As revelation comes to your heart,
and God allows you to see,
answers to your wise petition,
so much better you'll be.

FEBRUARY 11

DIVINE PROTECTION

Reading the newspaper,
you'll notice bad news,
of how people were hurt,
and didn't know what to do.

The television reveals,
coverage of crimes,
throughout the year,
all the time.

Random or planned,
murder or rape,
what would you do,
to prevent this fate?

Plead the blood,
everyday.
Speak His promises,
in what you say.

Claim protection,
in Jesus' name,
and for your family,
do the same.

Keep peril away,
from your home.
Listen to the words,
of this poem.

Don't be a victim,
of crimes so mean.
Be well aware,
of the devil's schemes.

Remember your covenant,
and speak words of faith,
to protect your household,
from crimes of hate.

FEBRUARY 12

UNTIE GOD'S HANDS

People often pray,
with sincere reverence,
hoping the answer will come,
with quick evidence.

Eyes of the physical,
say look and see.
Where's the answer,
is one's plea.

No quick answer,
so doubt arrives,
creating wavering,
amid the sighs.

The boat is rocked,
and fear sets in,
creating loss of confidence,
deep within.

God did fail,
so it would appear,
but that's not so,
please do hear.

Doubt and fear,
expressed through talk,
tied God's hands,
and affected your walk.

Eyes of the spirit,
have a different story,
one of faith,
and not of worry.

Let your words confirm,
and actions proclaim,
trusting for the answer,
in time you'll claim.

Remain steadfast,
and trust in God's Word.
Your prayer wasn't in vain,
be assured God heard.

Set your face like flint,
and refuse to waver.
It will manifest in time,
a moment you'll savor.

FEBRUARY 13

REACH FOR THE GUSTO

Reach for the gusto,
and enjoy your beer.
You only go around once,
is what you hear.

Make sure you party,
and party well.
Your friends will love it,
and think you're swell.

Turn up that music,
it's time to rock.
Rebel against the system,
and ensure you mock.

You only go around once,
so get on down.
Enjoy that music,
enjoy that sound.

Light a joint,
and breath real deep.
Reach for the gusto,
you sure are neat.

Tomorrow is later,
so live for now,
time to enjoy life,
and show them how.

The world promotes,
and clearly speaks,
but there's a better course,
one should seek.

Fruits will show,
you were deceived,
but there's a better choice,
you can receive.

Faith, love and peace,
can now be yours.
They're not counterfeit,
they're for sure.

Come to Jesus,
and reach for the gusto.
Enjoy life now,
and then to Heaven you'll go.

FEBRUARY 14

TEDDY BEARS

Teddy bears are seen,
throughout children's rooms.
Reasons exist,
I would assume.

A child will cling,
and clutch real tight,
to their teddy bear,
throughout the night.

Security is found,
with imagined love,
generating a comparison,
with God above.

God is love.
The Bible is clear,
that He's a good God,
one so dear.

God loves us,
with such a deep love.
That's why Jesus came,
sent from above.

Security is found,
in His Name.
Come to the Lord Jesus,
you'll never be the same.

Comfort you'll find,
in all situations.
He won't let you down,
He has covenant obligations.

Let Him embrace you,
with His arms.
He has your best interest,
and never will harm.

He'll fill that void,
that is within,
and walk closely with you,
and be your best friend.

Stay with Him,
and when you do,
you'll find his love not imagined,
but oh, so true.

FEBRUARY 15

HE FOUND YOU

People will say,
that they found God.
When I hear these words,
I find it odd.

They say they were searching,
to fill the space,
that was within their hearts,
when they found His grace.

Let's take some time,
of a sample case,
and review his past,
before he found God's grace.

Twelve years before,
this man received salvation,
this man was approached,
in friendly visitation.

He was given a tract,
that told him of God's love.
Although he didn't realize,
this was orchestrated from above.

The tract was nice,
and the words alright,
but at that particular time,
he refused God outright.

Over the years,
other events were arranged,
to try and reach his heart,
using related things.

It was during these tuggings,
God was doing His part,
when the man finally accepted,
Jesus into his heart.

FEBRUARY 16

FRUIT TREES

Walking through orchards,
will help you see,
wonderful fruit trees,
made for you and me.

You'll quickly notice,
that many types exist.
I actually suppose,
there's quite a list.

Apples, oranges, peaches,
or some other kind,
you'll see a consistent pattern,
a noticeable sign.

Fruit they produce,
this is true,
but let me help you,
and give you a clue.

It's easy to figure,
in your mind,
that fruit trees produce,
after their kind.

If people look,
they will learn,
a simple lesson here,
it's easy to discern.

People produce fruit,
in a similar way.
You'll notice it,
by watching each day.

Their fruit speaks loud,
and here's the key,
by observing them,
you'll know their tree.

FEBRUARY 17

STEER YOUR SHIP

Navigating the ocean,
has challenges indeed,
staying on the right course,
good direction must heed.

Currents are there,
they cannot be denied.
One must account for them,
and on a good course abide.

Watch coral reefs,
and sandbars too,
they're also there,
in the ocean blue.

Keep a watch,
in the middle of night.
Watch ships passing,
and keep them in sight.

Choices in life,
will flash detours,
often very attractive,
appealing with lures.

Maintain your guard,
and reference your chart.
It's your Bible,
guide for your heart.

Steer your course,
and steer it well.
Maintain your bearings,
as you sail.

Remain steadfast,
sure you can,
through all the storms,
you'll come to land.

FEBRUARY 18

TWO PLUS TWO EQUALS FOUR

I propose simple math.
Two plus two equals four.
This is a simple truth,
but there's more.

More answers can exist,
to that equation.
Listen closely,
as I build this foundation.

One could say five,
or even seven,
or how about six,
or even eleven.

They would be wrong,
it's easy to see,
for two is the answer,
it can only be.

Now here's the truth,
I want you to see.
One must accept Jesus,
to get Heaven's key.

Many choices are there,
but only one is true.
The others are false,
perhaps you knew.

Many religions exist,
there sure are many,
but there's a correct choice,
among the plenty.

The Bible states clearly,
it does say,
that through the blood of Jesus,
is the only way.

The path is narrow,
don't be deceived,
receive Jesus into your heart,
and only believe.

Truth is truth,
why say more,
so make the correct choice,
and unlock Heaven's door.

FEBRUARY 19

THE TRINITY

Water exists as a liquid,
only one of its states.
It can exist in two others,
make no mistake.

Change the temperature,
and make it cold,
then it becomes ice,
of which you can hold.

Turn up the heat,
and it changes more,
becoming a vapor,
upwards it soars.

Three states exist,
but molecules the same,
they only change,
in the form of name.

Think of this,
when considering the Trinity.
All three exist,
and have deity.

There's God the Father,
and God the Son,
and God the Holy Spirit,
deity in each one.

The Trinity is real,
to be a fact.
The Bible is clear,
it doesn't lack.

Reverence is in order,
when you approach deity.
Remember this,
when you consider the Trinity.

FEBRUARY 20

A STRONG BRIDGE

Girders of steel,
and slabs of concrete,
are often used,
with other ingredients.

To make a bridge,
and link the road,
built real strong,
to carry loads.

Designed against hazards,
it's built to protect,
ensuring that safety,
and connection is met.

Sin did come,
from the serpent's hand,
out of Eden,
separating God and man.

Man fell,
and broke God's law,
but God had a plan,
for He foresaw.

Jesus came,
to die on the cross,
shedding His blood,
for all the lost.

Jesus took man's hand,
and reached the throne,
offering His blood,
to bring us home.

A bridge was built,
from His sinless life,
relinking man to God,
through His supreme sacrifice.

FEBRUARY 21

CHECK YOUR DIET

Nourishment is needed,
from physical food.
A very poor diet,
will affect your moods.

Not enough good food,
and too much sweets,
in reality,
is not real neat.

The body will feel,
adverse effects,
when proper nutrition,
is not met.

The same is true,
in the spiritual realm,
without good food,
your walk will dim.

Check your menu,
on a daily routine,
and nourish your spirit,
to keep it keen.

Receive good teaching,
and read the Word.
Water the seeds,
of what you heard.

Mix some prayer,
with worship and praise,
and you'll notice a difference,
throughout all your days.

Eat good food,
and avoid the wrong.
Guard your heart,
and you'll grow real strong.

FEBRUARY 22

DISPLAY WINDOWS

Department stores use,
display windows well,
attracting people,
on products to dwell.

Get their attention,
as they pass near,
sell your products,
and make them dear.

Attractive they are,
both day or night,
as people look closely,
at products in sight.

Christians take note,
of these words,
and pay attention,
to what you heard.

People are looking,
both day and night,
and watching you closely,
and keeping you in sight.

A witness you are,
wherever you go.
You're on display,
you should know.

What do they see,
when they look at you,
a product to buy,
what do they do?

Your life does count,
wherever you go.
Sell your product well,
and maintain your glow.

FEBRUARY 23

INFRARED LIGHT

Infrared scopes,
when used at night,
allows one to see,
infrared light.

Not normally seen,
with the naked eye,
it does exist,
one does not deny.

The spiritual world,
it does exist.
It deserves some attention,
I don't want you to miss.

Infrared light exists,
evidence doesn't lack,
so does the spiritual realm,
to be a fact.

You may not see,
with your physical sight,
but in the color spectrum,
is infrared light.

Now you may doubt,
that spirits exist,
but that would be wrong,
and even remiss.

Don't be fooled,
by only physical sight,
but believe these words,
and receive some light.

The Bible is clear,
and does so state,
that spirits exist,
make no mistake.

God is a spirit,
and so is the devil.
Don't forget about angels,
or other demons of evil.

Man has a spirit,
that will live forever,
in Heaven or Hell.
Never say never.

FEBRUARY 24

BE A GOOD FARMER

Seeds are planted,
with some toil,
into the ground,
and covered with soil.

Add some water,
with the sun,
protect the seeds,
you're still not done.

Keep varmints out,
along with weeds,
then keep watering,
your good seeds.

Soon you'll see,
your crop take sprout.
You've maintained it well,
have no doubt.

Your heart is your garden,
and I will show,
that if you watch over it,
your harvest will grow.

Seeds are promises,
from God's Word,
planted in your heart,
good things you've heard.

Watering cultivates faith,
it makes good sense.
It means to keep hearing,
that's present tense.

Sunlight promotes growth,
and helps the seeds.
It equates to praise, thanksgiving and worship,
important deeds.

Guarding against varmints and weeds,
is necessary,
for they represent the devil,
your adversary.

The devil has strategies,
and tools indeed,
to affect your heart,
and rob your seeds.

So be on your guard,
and do be wise.
Grow your harvest,
and resist the devil's tries.

Help it grow,
to a hundred fold.
Be a good farmer,
as you've been told.

FEBRUARY 25

THE SWORD

Sharp it is,
made of steel,
a formidable weapon,
it could kill.

Used years ago,
in battles past,
its lethal history,
clearly lasts.

The Sword of the Spirit,
is mighty indeed,
to promote good works,
and accomplish good deeds.

Yield its power,
its backed by the Lord,
to combat forces of evil,
it's a mighty sword.

Decree the Word,
and take the offense.
Aggressive in speech,
is a great defense.

Know your weapon,
and what it can do.
It'll bring victory,
and see you through.

The defeated foe,
cannot stand,
the Word of God,
used by a born again man.

The Sword of the Spirit,
is one of your rights.
So take aim on the enemy,
and put him to flight.

FEBRUARY 26

THE DEVIL AND THE RUG

The resurrection was important,
when Christ rose again,
for He conquered Hell and the grave,
and redeemed man.

Authority was taken,
from Adam in the garden,
but God had a plan,
from Lucifer it was hidden.

Jesus left Heaven,
from His majestic seat,
to deliver a blow,
and seal Satan's defeat.

Victory was planned,
to come from the cross,
to set man free,
and save the lost.

Authority was retaken,
by Jesus that day,
but listen closely,
I have more to say.

Jesus delegated it to man,
before He ascended,
giving man authority,
it hasn't been amended.

So when the devil comes,
and knocks on your door,
just point to your feet,
or to the floor.

He's now like the rug,
that's under your feet,
forever defeated,
by Jesus' great feat.

Get this truth,
down in your spirit,
and when the devil comes near,
let him hear it.

Victory is ours,
for you and me.
So let's use our authority,
we've been set free.

FEBRUARY 27

THE GIFT

The package looks good,
all neatly wrapped,
and on the top,
with bow it's capped.

A gift it is,
prepared so well,
designed to make one,
feel so swell.

Now it's given,
by one so kind,
wanting to please,
with love in mind.

Freely it's handed,
with good intent,
to bring smiles,
to one it's sent.

People are pleased,
by gifts of man,
but consider a greater gift,
from God's own hand.

Salvation it is,
to be certain,
eternal life,
beyond life's curtain.

It's wrapped with grace,
and capped with love,
sent to earth,
from God above.

God sent His Son,
to die for the lost,
shedding His blood,
on the cross.

Life in Heaven,
will be so grand,
a gift available,
for each man.

The gift is there,
it's on your doorstep.
Jesus is asking,
will you accept?

FEBRUARY 28

STAND IN LINE

Plan on Disneyland,
it sounds like fun,
but bring a hat,
to shade the sun.

Plan on Magic Mountain,
it has great appeal.
All its rides,
sure do thrill.

Amusement parks,
sure are fine.
They're now everywhere,
in this time.

People drive miles,
from homes they depart,
and pay quite well,
to enter these parks.

Get in line,
and stand and wait.
It's only an hour,
to this ride's gate.

Careful as you exit,
hope you're satisfied,
after two minutes,
on this short ride.

Ride after ride,
it goes like this,
so stand in line,
you don't want to miss.

Hours and hours,
are spent in line,
but for church on Sunday,
there just isn't time.

What does the Lord think,
as He hears these replies,
excuse after excuse,
or are they just lies?

What's wrong with this picture,
please tell me?
May their eyes be open,
so they may see.

FEBRUARY 29

BE A MOUTHPIECE FOR JESUS

Christians must understand,
that they have important roles to play.
Their attitude towards the gospel,
will determine the words they say.

Christians must understand,
that the gospel comes without apology.
Truth is of great importance,
it's part of God's policy.

Christians must understand,
that lives are at stake,
and the importance of sharing,
with great effort to make.

Christians must understand,
the power of God's story,
and not to be hindered,
by shyness and worry.

Christians must be bold,
when led by God's Spirit,
to share the gospel with others,
and let them hear it.

Christians must understand,
their roles in these last days.
They must boldly speak for God,
with His Words to say.

The gospel is good news,
and it's meant for all mankind.
Start beginning to share,
for there's no better time.

Be a mouthpiece for Jesus,
and share His Word.
You may be surprised,
that some have never heard.

MARCH 1

COME TO THE SHOW

The theater provides movies,
and even plays,
different programs,
on different days.

People get excited,
about a good show,
and will check listings,
before they go.

Color and costumes,
they're all there,
so is choreography,
it's handled with care.

No matter how great,
the entertainment seems,
I know of a better show,
that will make you beam.

God has a show,
that He has planned.
It will last forever,
and involve redeemed man.

The goodness of God's grace,
on display it will be,
as He reveals to the saints,
wonders throughout eternity.

Tickets are available,
to be part of this deal,
but to come to this show,
by blood it's sealed.

A ticket is yours,
if you accept God's Son.
Don't die without Him,
or then there'll be none.

This show is coming,
and it will be great.
Don't wait too long,
or even hesitate.

Come to Jesus,
receive your pass,
and be part of the show,
that will ever last.

MARCH 2

SCHOOL PRAYER

Ministers lead Congressmen,
in prayer at inaugurations,
bowing their heads,
before the nation.

The President's term,
it's about to begin.
Let's seek God's help,
and ask Him to send.

It's a Christian nation,
under God,
but consider school prayer,
before you nod.

Our leaders bow,
in quiet reverence,
but for school prayer,
there has been severance.

Unconstitutional,
the leaders say,
to start school in prayer,
at the beginning of each day.

Leaders have determined,
to prayer confine,
limiting it to ceremonies,
which would be fine.

Lead by example,
and dare to be bold.
Don't worry about votes,
and let this be told.

If God is real,
as you lead this democracy,
then begin to act like it,
and drop the hypocrisy.

On Christian principles,
this nation was found,
to shy from God's Word,
will cause shaky ground.

Many special groups,
have false interpretations,
so stay with the Bible,
to have a strong nation.

MARCH 3

IS IT A CHILD?

A child is born,
prematurely.
Many cases happen daily,
or even yearly.

As it is saved,
there is celebration,
and rightly so,
this isn't aberration.

The doctor proclaims,
a child is here,
born at seven months,
she looks so dear.

Down the road,
there's a different story,
of a fetus taken,
no need to worry.

The said abortion,
has now taken place.
It was only seven months,
there's no disgrace.

More tissue for research,
has now come.
It's starting to add up,
there's quite a sum.

It can be used,
in makeup too,
dollars from cosmetics,
what a coup.

Two different stories,
and two different cases,
consider them both,
without making haste.

Is it a child,
my question to thee?
Please think wisely,
before you answer me.

MARCH 4

COMPASS AND MAP

One can navigate,
and in terrain adapt,
with the help of a compass,
and a good map.

Plan your route,
know your declination,
and don't forget,
about your variation.

You're on a ridge,
you're doing fine,
but a valley is coming,
in a short time.

High you were,
but now you're low.
Don't stop now,
many miles to go.

Maintain your bearing,
crossing that creek,
and keep your cool,
in that heat.

A fork in the road,
is now in sight,
which way to go,
which way is right.

Check your map,
and compass trust,
maintain your bearing,
it's a must.

So what's the moral,
of these words?
Translate clearly,
what I've heard.

Life is full,
of decisions to make,
making the right ones,
is for your sake.

Changes occur,
throughout life's years.
Sometimes situations,
are not so dear.

Guidance is needed,
to stay on course,
and the following advice,
I will endorse.

The map is the Bible,
and the compass His promises.
Now listen closely,
and don't be a doubting Thomas.

Read the Bible,
and know what it says,
and speak His promises,
throughout all your days.

No matter what decisions,
or hard questions,
trust in God's Word,
in all situations.

Through life's swamps,
it'll bring you through.
It'll provide light for you,
in all you do.

So use your map,
and compass too.
Set your course,
in all you do.

MARCH 5

HEARTBEAT

An important organ,
is the heart.
It pumps life's blood,
throughout all life's parts.

Great work is done,
with each beat.
Pumping gallons of blood,
a continuous schedule it keeps.

Its work is often,
well overlooked,
but it's very industrious,
just look in a book.

No replacement exists,
that can truly replace,
the functions required,
and keep its pace.

Models may try,
and models may prolong,
but often just temporary,
until they go wrong.

When the heartbeat stops,
and there are no more,
one will proceed,
to one of two doors.

Those in Christ,
will go to Heaven's gate,
for all of them,
an important date.

Those unsaved,
will see a different veil,
when they are ushered,
to the entrance of Hell.

Life is short,
compared to eternity,
so receive Christ,
and join Heaven's fraternity.

The spiritual life,
is just a heartbeat away.
You'll enjoy Heaven,
if you are saved.

MARCH 6

FLY FREE

There was some flooding up ahead,
and traffic was jammed.
A storm had suddenly come in,
and hit the town.

I turned my head in frustration,
towards the direction of the coast.
I then spotted a bird,
that was on a fence post.

He got my attention,
as his head turned my way.
He then taught me a lesson,
with a few words to say.

The little bird spoke to me,
just before he flew.
He said in my flight,
there's a message for you.

Moving his wings,
he prepared to take flight.
He then lifted his wings,
and flew out of sight.

What could this mean,
were my first thoughts.
Then the lesson struck home,
and in my heart was caught.

Fly free from your worries,
you don't have to stay where you are.
He was referring to life,
as I pondered in my car.

The Lord states in His Word,
to give all your cares to Him.
We are to fly free of their hold,
and He'll handle all of them.

MARCH 7

MASQUERADE BLUES

People often wear masks,
at costume or social events.
Many consider it fun,
at these festive events.

It may appear fun,
but underneath these facades,
exist many lonely souls,
that are living without God.

In their real lives,
they also wear masks.
Many feign contentment,
but they're really downcast.

There's a void within,
that they seek to fill,
as they go through life,
trying out different thrills.

Their souls cry out,
to be redeemed,
from their current state,
of silent screams.

Many don't realize,
what they're searching for,
is really the Lord Jesus,
which is God's cure.

The void is real,
but God will fill it.
If you come to Him,
He'll take care of it.

Take off the mask,
and give up the masquerade blues.
Jesus is waiting,
but you must choose.

MARCH 8

THE UMPIRE

Baseball games are played,
throughout the land.
Most people know how,
each to a man.

Three bases there are,
and a pitcher's mound.
Crowds often cheer,
creating great sound.

Behind home plate,
the umpire stands,
calling balls and strikes,
with his hands.

The umpire affects the game,
as he makes the calls.
Influencing the outcome,
he sets the law.

Life has decisions,
that must be made.
Now here's a tip,
that will surely aid.

To your heart,
look this day,
and listen closely,
to what I say.

Your heart has a voice,
it's your spirit,
and will help you,
if you'll follow it.

The peace of God,
should clearly reign,
in your spirit,
over things.

If peace exists,
then that's a good sign,
if it doesn't,
you're probably out of line.

Let peace be your umpire,
as you go forth.
So look to your spirit,
and maintain your course.

MARCH 9

P.O.W.

P.O.W. stands for prisoner of war.
It's a common term,
that throughout our society,
many have learned.

It's important to learn from history,
most will agree.
So let's examine a story,
with great value to see.

Man was held captive,
in the bondage of sin.
Satan stood guard,
against the freedom of man.

God had a plan,
that Satan did not know.
It was decided that Jesus,
to earth He would go.

Born in Bethlehem,
in the form of man,
Jesus commenced his operation,
that would gain freedom for man.

With clandestine intrigue,
his life evolved.
Many times Satan was confused,
over this operation unsolved.

Time on target,
was recorded at the cross,
when Jesus gave His life,
for all the lost.

No guns or bullets,
could be seen,
but power was at work,
in the unseen.

The raid was successful,
when God freed the lost.
Man was set free,
and bondage cast off.

No longer a P.O.W.,
man was now set free.
Walk out of your cell,
and receive Christ's victory.

MARCH 10

LITTLE FOXES

The vine grows grapes,
they develop in time,
but little foxes come,
and spoil the vine.

One prays in prayer,
but the answer is slow,
causing one to ponder,
and want to know.

One must begin,
to examine one's heart,
and look real closely,
at each part.

Is unforgiveness there?
Take a look.
It affects one's prayer,
it's in God's Book.

After one has prayed,
is there doubt?
If there is,
then get it out.

After one has prayed,
is there fear?
It's the opposite of faith,
and to God not dear.

With your spouse,
is there strife?
Then deal with it,
for your prayer life.

Check yourself,
and how you've talked,
words you've spoken,
on your walk.

Negative words,
have an affect.
So guard your mouth,
and do not neglect.

Find the little foxes,
and send them away,
then check your vine,
for harvest day.

MARCH 11

IN THE LIONS' DEN

Daniel was thrown,
into the lions' den,
protected by an angel,
that God did send.

Daniel trusted God,
as he was there,
for the lions came near,
down in their liar.

The lions were there,
their teeth were real,
but as Daniel stood,
their mouths were sealed.

Trials do come,
they do exist.
They come with living,
they're hard to miss.

Pray to God,
when heat is there.
Don't get worried,
from the scare.

Know that God,
wants you blessed,
as He helped Daniel,
through his mess.

God is with you,
when you stand,
to walk you through,
hand in hand.

So trials will come,
you should know,
but God goes with you,
wherever you go.

MARCH 12

CHECK YOUR WELL

In rural America,
many wells were dug,
to provide water,
that had to be lugged.

Wells were the source,
of their life's water,
taken from the ground,
into their quarters.

Wells were important,
for water to supply,
and drew immediate attention,
if they went dry.

People looked elsewhere,
if this was the case,
for a better area,
with much haste.

Digging would take place,
in other ground,
for a better source,
where water could be found.

To this I say,
God's Word is alive,
and with similar tenacity,
one must strive.

Check your church house,
and if it is dead,
then find another house,
that's Holy Spirit led.

For each of us,
God has a place,
to teach and encourage us,
in the shadow of grace.

As many will look,
for an abundant well,
so it should be,
for a good church to dwell.

Spiritual truth is important,
to receive into one's heart,
so get to the right place,
and do your part.

MARCH 13

BE YE HOLY

Be ye holy,
the Word does say.
It's not an option,
come what may.

Notice in the Word,
this is direction.
If you think otherwise,
you need correction.

To ignore these words,
is to play with sin.
To the Holy Spirit,
do not offend.

What does this mean,
you may ask within.
Well, to start with,
you must abhor sin.

Walk in obedience,
to His revelation.
Be willing to change,
and accept His direction.

A reverence for God,
must come into play,
where it's a daily walk,
day after day.

In all areas of our life,
God wants purity.
It's part of holiness,
and should be priority.

So get eyes off the world,
this shouldn't sound odd,
and passionately seek Him,
and the things of God.

MARCH 14

HEART'S CRY

People have desires,
that burn within,
sometimes with great passion,
that never end.

Some desires vary,
from man to man,
for people are different,
throughout the land.

When a desire is met,
and becomes fulfilled,
one typically reacts,
with great thrill.

The feeling is grand,
with much pleasure derived.
It makes one feel great,
about being alive.

All folks can relate,
and with this identify,
for when a desire is met,
it certainly satisfies.

The Father has desires,
I want you to know.
Just by looking into the Bible,
it would be easy to show.

One desire really stands out,
and is so crystal clear.
It's the salvation of souls,
that God holds so dear.

The heart cry of the Father,
continually calls out,
for the salvation of souls,
of this don't doubt.

Salvation of souls,
make no mistake,
is the Father's heart cry,
that is so great.

The salvation of a soul,
brings great satisfaction,
to the heart of the Father,
with great jubilation.

MARCH 15

WHEAT KERNELS

The wheat field at harvest time,
provides an interesting sight,
where wheat heads can be seen,
and provide some spiritual light.

Some wheat heads can be seen,
standing straight and erect,
while others appear more bowed,
as if from neglect.

One may perceive,
upon first glance,
that the erect have wheat kernels,
from their stance.

Take another look,
and don't be deceived,
for it's the bowed ones,
so listen to receive.

Some people are extremely proud,
and will stand straight and erect,
of some you may know,
and have actually met.

They'll stand out,
and act with arrogant pride.
Observe their demeanor,
if you stand beside.

Now consider others,
of humility stance,
and observe more closely,
with more than a glance.

Kindhearted and respectful,
you will quickly observe,
the way they treat others,
and the way they serve.

The attitude of humility,
contains the kernels of wheat.
It's the stronger of the two,
and certainly not weak.

The attitudes are different,
it's easy to see.
So let us ask ourselves,
which one have we?

MARCH 16

GUARD AGAINST GREED

There was a greedy rich man,
who looked all around him.
He saw people in great need.
There were many of them.

He then looked into an old mirror,
made of glass with a silver coat.
Words then came to his mind,
that his heart spoke.

Add silver to that glass,
and you see only yourself.
It made him consider his values,
that he had within himself.

He then thought how when people die,
that they leave all of their possessions.
Perhaps in that old mirror,
was an important lesson.

No matter how great,
goods can't be taken.
His priorities in life,
now were shaken.

His needs were met,
with more than enough.
Abundance was his,
with all sorts of stuff.

Selfish he was,
but greed must be broken.
It came from his heart,
inner words that were spoken.

As he began to bless others,
he noticed their smiles,
and began to feel better,
preferring this style.

Rewarding it was,
as he began to perceive,
that giving was better,
and in turn he received.

Live for this world,
and you'll go out a poor man.
Bless others on the way,
and you'll die a rich man.

MARCH 17

COMMITMENT COUNTS

Christianity came to America,
many years ago,
which can be traced to Silas and Paul,
and the seeds they did sow.

Come to Macedonia,
the vision did call,
and forward they went,
both Silas and Paul.

To jail they were thrown,
in the town of Philippi,
for preaching the gospel,
which they proposed no alibi.

Then the ground did shake,
and the shackles came free,
with the jailer becoming fearful,
and afraid to see.

The jailer was about to take his life,
thinking the prisoners had escaped,
but Paul and Silas called out,
before it was too late.

They led the jailer to Christ,
and his family as well.
Now others were available,
to spread the gospel and tell.

From here the gospel spread,
to Europe and other lands,
all because of the commitment,
of these two willing men.

Commitment does count.
So be appraised,
that your actions are important,
and affect many lives.

MARCH 18

I CHOOSE

Decisions are made,
when one does choose.
It's a matter of choice,
that one does do.

Chocolate or vanilla,
which one will it be?
It's a matter of choice,
this is easy to see.

As you get good teaching,
from the Word,
then you must choose,
to do what you heard.

Do not be a hearer only,
this will not suffice,
but also be a doer,
if you want some sound advice.

"I choose to bless others."
The Word does say,
that would be a good one,
to practice today.

"I choose to walk in faith."
Make no mistake,
this is a good decision,
for you to make.

"I choose to walk in love."
Our Heavenly Father above,
is always pleased,
to see us walk in love.

"I choose to forgive."
Choosing to forgive,
and not to hold grudges,
is the better way to live.

The choice is yours,
to be a doer of the Word,
or to choose not to do,
and to disregard what you've heard.

Now that you've read this,
I expect you've surmised,
the recommended choices,
that would be wise.

MARCH 19

STOP LIGHTS

Stop lights change colors.
Green means go,
while red does the opposite,
and stops traffic flow.

Amber means caution,
and lets people know,
that they must prepare to stop,
and begin to slow.

An analogy can be made,
with man's spirit,
if we'll look its way,
and listen to it.

Your spirit will help,
and serve as a guide,
to make the right decisions,
for it's on your side.

As you listen closely,
it may say,
don't make that choice,
and go that way.

The tug will be there,
at other times,
to tell you to move forward,
with a go sign.

Approach with caution,
may also be perceived,
as it sends these words,
for you to receive.

Listen to your spirit,
it will guide you right,
to help you make the best decisions,
during day or night.

MARCH 20

KELP

When diving off the west coast,
a diver knows,
that beds of kelp,
do certainly grow.

As he dives,
and swims through them,
he must watch for tangling,
around his limbs.

He must be careful,
and look and see,
when diving through them,
to remain free.

Things will tangle,
as kelp in one's life,
and it can all begin,
with arguing and strife.

Anger tangles,
you better believe,
and of its fruits,
you don't want to receive.

Bitterness tangles,
you should know,
so pull out at its roots,
and don't allow it to grow.

Jealousy tangles,
and traps the mind,
into wrong acts,
much of the time.

Unforgiveness tangles,
and provides no perk,
for if harbored,
it will truly hurt.

Disappointment tangles,
you have to move on,
so put it behind you,
and consider it gone.

An anecdote exists,
that I will prescribe,
get into God's Word,
and in your heart do hide.

MARCH 21

OXYGEN

Oxygen is required,
for man to live.
Into the lungs it's drawn,
from the air that gives.

Essential to the blood,
make no mistake,
the body uses it well,
with each breath it takes.

Without oxygen,
the body dies.
It's an essential element,
for the body to survive.

Your spirit needs something else,
and oxygen isn't it,
but it's just as essential,
made for your spirit.

The Word of God,
it is alive.
It's the oxygen of your spirit,
that helps it to survive.

If your spirit never receives it,
it will surely die.
I tell you the truth,
and do not lie.

A substitute for oxygen doesn't exist.
It's the same with the Bible,
as it relates to your spirit man,
and its survival.

With each breath,
consider what you heard,
and let it serve as a reminder,
to get in the Word.

MARCH 22

QUITTERS DO WIN

Winners never quit.
I certainly like this phrase,
but quitters do win,
depending on the phase.

During some phases,
some may go astray,
causing havoc in their lives,
with much dismay.

The ravages of sin,
will take their toll,
attacking as a storm,
that's bitter and cold.

Give up the adultery,
or give up the drugs.
Turn back to the Lord,
and receive His hugs.

Give up the indifference,
or give up the greed.
Whatever it is,
take the Lord's lead.

Break free from sin,
and get away from its clutch.
Run to the Father,
Who loves you so much.

In reference to quitters,
they certainly do win,
when they return to the Lord,
and repent of their sin.

When you turn from sin,
and jump over its hurdle,
you cross victory's line,
into the winner's circle.

MARCH 23

THE SCARLET CORD

The Israelites told,
Rahab the Harlot,
to tie a cord in the window,
that was to be colored scarlet.

When the Israelites came,
against Jericho's walls,
there was the scarlet cord,
that the Israelites saw.

Rahab and her family,
protected they were,
from the Israelite assault,
as if they weren't there.

The scarlet cord,
serves as symbology,
when compared to Christ's blood,
in an interesting analogy.

The scarlet blood of Jesus,
forgives and protects,
much as the scarlet cord,
that was tied without neglect.

There's power in the blood,
to forgive and protect,
but it must be received and applied,
without slightest neglect.

In the blood of Jesus,
there is power indeed,
to confront any situation,
and to meet every need.

Thank God for the blood,
that was shed for you and me.
Let us use it in our lives,
as we benefit from Christ's victory.

MARCH 24

LIMBURGER CHEESE

A very tired man,
decided to take a nap.
It was in a reclining chair,
where he sat.

A prankster came by,
and rubbed some limburger cheese,
into the man's shirt pocket,
where one could hardly see.

The man awoke,
and said the room stunk,
and so he left quickly,
as if he smelled a skunk.

To the kitchen he went,
and the result was the same.
He proclaimed the kitchen unfit,
and departed without blame.

To the dining room he went,
and was heard to exclaim,
that the room stunk,
with an animated scream.

Outside he went,
with the smell on his clothes,
and then he noticed,
it was right under his nose.

A person who criticizes,
and goes from church to church,
perhaps should pause,
and take a look at his shirt.

A finger is pointed,
and the smell proclaimed,
but maybe the odor comes from elsewhere,
where there should be blame.

Take a look at your attitude,
and monitor your words.
Do they match this story,
and what you just heard?

If this is the case,
then look under your nose,
and check for the smell,
that comes from your clothes.

MARCH 25

UNCLAIMED TREASURE

Treasure excites people,
I'm sure you'll agree.
Just the thought of finding it,
brings most people glee.

It's easy to appreciate,
reactions like this,
when people express happiness,
and feelings of bliss.

Yet nuggets of gold,
are before peoples' eyes,
as they choose to ignore them,
with the saddest of sighs.

The nuggets are available,
but there they sit,
as people walk over them,
and won't even kick.

The promises of the Bible,
are these nuggets of gold,
that many people won't receive,
even though they've been told.

The promises are real,
and they come with power,
to cover health and prosperity,
and other needs in this hour.

Due to lack of knowledge,
people will perish.
It's a common occurrence,
whether church or parish.

I have to emphasize,
and make this clear.
There's unclaimed treasure,
that to you is near.

Reach down and pick it up,
to you I plead,
and you'll find out,
it'll meet all your needs.

Don't ignore the nuggets,
and make God wonder why,
why you didn't lay claim,
but chose to deny.

MARCH 26

WALK ON THE WATER

Walk on the water,
and thus Peter obeyed,
as Jesus spoke to him,
before his eyes would stray.

Peter's eyes were fixed,
from the very start,
on the words of Jesus,
as he begin to debark.

Peter actually walked,
step by step,
before he looked at the seas,
and cried out for help.

It can be easily observed,
that things were fine,
before Peter looked at the circumstances,
and got into a bind.

Walk he did,
this cannot be denied,
as he focused on Jesus,
and of his words complied.

Then his attention strayed,
and he started to doubt,
even though he was walking,
and of the boat was out.

Focus on Jesus,
and trust in His Word,
for circumstances will speak loud,
against what you just heard.

Walk on the water,
though waves may surge.
Resist doubt and fear,
and don't give in to their urge.

Walk on the water.
Though winds may blow,
as you trust in Jesus,
with you He'll go.

Walk on the water.
Though storms may come,
as you trust in Jesus,
you'll see the sun.

MARCH 27

BE LIKE A DOG

As I approached,
I heard Max bark.
He knew it was me,
even in the dark.

He came to meet me,
at the front door,
jumping to and fro,
around the floor.

His face was fixed,
for my attention,
awaiting my touch,
and recognition.

I could easily tell,
he missed me much,
as he reacted,
from my touch.

Wagging his tail,
he let me know,
he wanted me near,
and not to go.

With words of love,
his eyes did talk,
as he followed me,
wherever I walked.

We can learn,
from little Max,
with his show of love,
he is not lax.

He gives me more,
than I could ask,
a genuine love,
with no mask.

I will say this,
perhaps you knew,
that he reaps my love,
you've seen the clue.

A lesson is here,
for us to heed,
if we'll learn from dogs,
and take their lead.

MARCH 28

TEMPLE OF GOD

Historical landmarks,
are usually maintained,
in good order,
and are properly cleaned.

One can easily say,
without reservation,
that they're treated well,
and have good preservation.

The grounds look good,
and the grass is trimmed.
It's usually the norm,
for most of them.

Respect is rendered,
as people look on,
observing the landmarks,
from lines often long.

A precious landmark,
although a mystery,
can be found with Christians,
in current history.

For those that are saved,
the body provides,
a place for Jesus,
to come and reside.

A Christian's body,
is a temple of God.
This shouldn't be taken lightly,
or considered odd.

Take care of your body,
and treat it well,
for it's where Jesus,
has come to dwell.

You take Jesus,
wherever you go.
This is a sobering thought,
that you should know.

You're a temple of God,
make no mistake,
so keep the grounds clean,
on your estate.

MARCH 29

SOMEONE SPECIAL

The world looks on,
and pays tribute,
to dressed up rock stars,
that make good loot.

Go to the stadium,
and check out sports.
You'll see homage,
to a wealthy sort.

Look at movies,
and check some starlets,
who gain fame,
by playing harlots.

The media helps,
to fan the flame,
helping many people,
to gain great fame.

World heroes,
if not Christians,
are not so special,
if you will listen.

Truly special people,
can be found indoors,
or you may find many of them,
even outdoors.

No need to guess,
or roll the dice,
for they're in that group,
that have accepted Christ,

They're sons of God,
saved by grace,
which makes them special,
in the human race.

All known by the Father,
but many not by the media,
you won't see many of them,
in the encyclopedia.

God's heroes,
differ from man's.
Guess who takes priority,
if you can.

MARCH 30

LOOK AND SEE

Lock the box.
Look and see,
as the magician gets out,
without a key.

See the cards,
in his hand.
Watch this trick,
what a man.

These are tricks,
designed to deceive,
but for them to work,
you must look and see.

See that growth,
on your arm.
Look and see,
it could cause harm.

See those bills,
on your desk.
Look and see,
you're in a real mess.

See that gal,
out at night.
Look and see,
what a sight.

With attention gained,
he'll work on your mind,
as you've given him rope,
and have crossed his line.

Look and see,
it looks real bad.
Now think real hard,
and become real sad.

Kill, steal and destroy.
It's the devil's theme,
as he uses deception,
in the realm of seen.

You know his game,
so resist his ploy.
Respond with the Word,
and retain your joy.

MARCH 31

HE WON'T BE LATE

A pattern of time,
exists in the physical,
and so it is,
in the realm of the spiritual.

The sun comes up,
and the sun goes down.
It's a daily occurrence,
around earth's ground.

Leaves fall in autumn,
followed by winter snow,
giving way to springtime,
and its dew of glow.

Clouds draw in vapor,
during times of heat,
and then release raindrops,
they cannot keep.

The trees grow up,
yielding fruit on limb.
Now the farmer can come,
and begin to pick them.

God has a timetable,
and is never late,
for His answer to prayer,
He has a date.

So when you kneel,
and begin to pray,
don't become frustrated,
if there is delay.

He knows the time,
and when to send.
So remain steadfast,
and refuse to bend.

In your time of need,
faithful is He.
As you wait for your answer,
in time you'll see.

Just trust in God,
and keep your faith,.
There is a time,
He won't be late.

APRIL 1

BOB THE SNOWMAN

Winter has come,
and snow is on the ground.
So let's build a snowman,
with three sections round.

Roll the snow,
and do a good job,
and when we're finished,
we'll name him Bob.

Stones for his eyes,
will do just fine.
Now check their level,
to ensure a good line.

Get a carrot,
for his nose,
and let us check,
for some clothes.

Place a hat,
on his crown,
and make him smile,
not with frown.

Get a scarf,
for his neck.
We're getting close.
We're almost set.

Now grab two sticks,
for his arms.
He sure looks swell,
and has a charm.

Spring is near,
and time has past.
The snow is melting,
and will not last.

Bob's life is gone,
just like that,
leaving just memories,
like his scarf and hat.

From the earth he came,
and to the earth he returned,
leaving us a truth,
that's easy to learn.

APRIL 2

SOURCE OF ALL BLESSINGS

A body of water,
usually has a source,
that feeds into it,
and supports its course.

Check mountain streams,
and if you will,
follow their leads,
down their hills.

In the end,
you'll often find,
a larger body of water,
most of the time.

Perhaps it's a lake,
or even a river,
but the source is important,
and must not be severed.

The source of all blessings,
comes from above.
It's a wonderful source,
our God of great love.

Blessings are important,
to the lives of man.
They improve quality of lives,
throughout earth's land.

Our Father is consistent,
He does not change.
He gives blessings of good,
and not gifts of pain.

Know the streams of the Father,
are your blessings source,
designed to help you,
along your life's course.

APRIL 3

I WAS THERE

The newsletter just covered,
a trip that was made,
to Central Africa,
to conduct a crusade.

Pictures were shown,
of people healed,
of deadly diseases,
that were designed to kill.

Hands were uplifted,
as people gave,
their hearts to Jesus,
and were saved.

I began to ponder,
the words of print,
and what transpired,
from offerings sent.

The gospel is free,
but it costs to send,
to get souls saved,
and redeemed from sin.

The power of prayer,
had a part,
to prepare the way,
and soften hearts.

People were healed,
and souls were saved,
because Christians gave,
and also prayed.

I was not there,
in a physical way,
but spiritually speaking,
I was there that day.

APRIL 4

FICKLE BEHAVIOR

Notice a child's attention,
when given a task.
The child starts off well,
but sometimes it doesn't last.

He means well at the start,
but do remain leery,
as his attention wanes,
or he becomes weary.

A child is fickle,
it's part of youth.
It takes him some time,
to develop more couth.

A child grows up,
to become an adult.
Hopefully he has matured,
with now different results.

Unfortunately we see,
this isn't always the case.
Just check out our society,
or your church home base.

People remain fickle,
and will turn on a dime.
Just look around you,
it's a sign of the times.

People attend church,
and will get on fire,
but just two weeks later,
they've lost their desire.

As people mature,
attitudes must grow,
as fickle behavior,
must be let go.

Commitment is important,
and must be applied,
if in God's Word,
one is to abide.

Be steadfast in the Lord,
and stay real strong.
Don't be fickle towards Him,
it would be wrong.

APRIL 5

FLY IN THE SOUP

The soup looks good,
and sure is hot.
Let's keep it stirred,
while in the pot.

It's time to serve,
now have a seat.
We're getting close,
it's time to eat.

Now help yourself,
to soup cuisine.
It has some beef,
that sure is lean.

Dainty morsels,
are in this meal,
but there's something else,
that comes with deal.

Check your soup,
and look real close.
There's something else,
from your host.

You'll see a fly,
in your bowl.
It's certainly there,
just like I told.

It's a recipe for gossip,
so do perceive,
the lesson taught,
and do receive.

When this soup is served,
just walk away,
and refuse to eat,
whatever day.

APRIL 6

ON THIN ICE

During the winter months,
to the creek we would go,
to skate on frozen ice,
surrounded by snow.

Shovels in hand,
with us we would take,
to clear some ice,
before we would skate.

Memories come back,
as I meditate,
of those childhood days,
that we would skate.

The ice had to be solid,
to hold our weight.
It's something we would check,
before we would skate.

Sometimes we would find,
to prevent a mess,
spots of ice,
that would not pass the test.

To skate on thin ice,
would not be wise.
Most people would agree,
and would not deny.

Many folks today,
are skating on thin ice.
They're living their lives,
like the rolling of dice.

Reckless living may break,
their skate on the ice,
with precarious results,
that aren't real nice.

Living for the world,
will have given them thrills,
but when it comes time to make payment,
they will have big bills.

In reference to Jesus,
they chose to neglect.
Then the piper will call,
and come to collect.

APRIL 7

TIME GOES BY

History is written,
with the passage of time.
Some chapters record travesty,
and some sublime.

As each second ticks,
it's gone forever,
not to be seen again,
which really means never.

What's done is done.
It's now in the past,
as decisions were made,
and fates were cast.

A measure of time,
is given to man,
to use as he will,
and pass as he can.

One can be rude,
or one can be civil.
One can do good,
or one can do evil.

One's use of time,
will have much affect,
on many lives,
with great effects.

One's life does count,
in the realm of the physical,
but perhaps more so,
in the realm of the spiritual.

Paul's missionary journeys,
were designed with goals,
to spread the gospel,
and to save men's souls.

Christianity came to America,
as a result of Paul's toil,
It was time well spent,
that brought the gospel to this soil.

Nations are changed,
as are individual lives.
So let's use our time wisely,
and for good impact strive.

APRIL 8

HOTEL STAY

Line up your room,
as you plan your trip,
and take the right clothes,
if you want a good tip.

It'll be a short stay,
and won't be long,
before you return,
and come on home.

Keep this in mind,
and stay in touch.
It's because of love,
that you're missed so much.

Get your key,
at the front desk,
and find the room,
to your brief nest.

Take care of business,
and become not attached,
to your temporary dwelling,
and to it not latch.

Know for certain,
you're going to leave,
and return on home,
where you will be.

Heaven is your home,
if you're in Christ.
You made it so,
when you gave Him your life.

A sojourner you are,
one might say,
as you've come to earth,
for just a short stay.

APRIL 9

PUMPING IRON

Put the bar on the bench,
and load it with weights.
Now lay on your back,
and bench press make.

Curls are next,
so get into position.
Commence your curl,
and do ten repetitions.

Keep on your schedule,
and you'll start to see signs,
of increased strength,
over a period of time.

Tone will improve,
along with definition,
as you've worked real hard,
to add muscle addition.

Exercise was required,
to build your physique.
Magic wasn't involved,
with some strange mystique.

Time and effort,
they were applied,
and from this fact,
you cannot hide.

To grow spiritually,
in a similar way,
requires time and effort,
throughout one's day.

Time in the Word,
and time with the Lord,
are the essential notes,
that strike the right chord.

APRIL 10

A PRETTY FACE

A pretty face,
can be easily found,
as you check the streets,
of most any town.

Visiting a salon,
can ensure one's hair,
is neatly fixed,
with style and flair.

Shapely figures,
can be found in view,
often together,
with a stylish hair-do.

Outside apparel,
can surely attract,
for those that dress,
with a certain knack.

Looks are fine,
don't get me wrong,
but inner beauty,
sings a better song.

A woman of God,
can radiate,
a wonderful glow,
that permeates.

It's an inner beauty,
that shines forth,
from the love of God,
which is her source.

Paint the barn,
if you will,
but feed your spirit,
to look better still.

APRIL 11

TWO CURTAINS

Curtain number one,
or curtain number two,
all get one choice,
no matter who.

Your choice must be made,
while life you breathe.
So choose wisely,
and don't be deceived.

Curtain number one,
provides a way,
to Heaven's land,
but you must be saved.

Curtain number two,
provides a way,
to Hell's land,
for those not saved.

Eternal life,
and the love of God,
await the saved,
on Heaven's sod.

Eternal torment,
and separation from God,
await the unsaved,
on Hell's sod.

Both curtains exist,
the choices are real.
So choose number one,
I do appeal.

All that glitters,
is not gold.
Don't buy Satan's lies,
and sell your soul.

God is so good,
and will treat you fine.
You can trust His promises,
all the time.

Two curtains there are.
You must choose one.
So what will it be?
I recommend God's Son.

APRIL 12

UTOPIA

To improve society,
has been a desire of man,
different approaches to Utopia,
throughout earth's land.

Throughout time,
of the world's history,
the achievement of Utopia,
has remained a mystery.

Better ways,
are continuously sought,
for all systems,
have problems fraught.

Flaws are found,
in all governments,
generated from man,
they're not Heaven sent.

It's because man has flesh,
and carnality exists,
that prevents realization,
and causes constant miss.

The search continues,
but it's as hard as beryllium,
for man will not find it,
until Christ's millennium.

Peace will flow,
as out of a cornucopia,
for Christ will reign,
during this Utopia.

Christ will show,
and help man see,
after thousands of years,
the way it should be.

APRIL 13

A TIME AS THIS

Mordecai approached Esther,
on that day,
and these are words,
that he did say.

You were born,
for a time as this,
so be faithful,
and do not miss.

Esther saved her people,
and defeated Haman,
as God used her,
in His masterful plan.

God has a plan,
for each of our lives,
and it's very important,
in God's eyes.

Your life,
is not insignificant.
So listen closely,
and don't be flippant.

You were born,
for a time as this.
There is a plan,
you're on God's list.

Sometimes you may think,
you were a mistake,
but things have been planned,
since your birth date.

People to see,
and appointments to keep,
there's rhyme and reason,
so don't sleep.

You have a part,
in life's great play.
So fill your role,
come what may.

Be always faithful.
Be always true,
as you follow God's plan,
in all you do.

APRIL 14

CHOOSE TO BELIEVE

You can choose to be happy,
or you can choose to be sad,
life is full of choices,
both good and bad.

Much of it depends,
on your matter of approach,
how you view things,
and how you were coached.

You made a choice,
when you accepted Christ.
It wasn't a matter,
of just throwing dice.

A decision was made,
as you followed through.
The principle is the same,
in all you do.

The promises of God,
are for those in Christ,
as you choose to believe,
which makes it nice.

So find a promise,
and take a stand,
to cover your situation,
as you look to God's hand.

You've made a choice,
you've chosen to believe.
Now begin to act like it,
and get ready to receive.

Believing God's promises,
will set you right.
Imagine the result,
and keep it in sight.

Speak words of faith,
and run your race.
Trust in God,
to send His grace.

It's easy to believe,
for you're a believer.
So rest in Him,
and become a receiver.

APRIL 15

YOU'RE A DEAD MAN

The old self died,
when you were born again,
as you were washed by the blood,
of all your sins.

At Calvary's cross,
you died that day.
Instant redemption,
there was no delay.

Dead to the flesh,
is my theme,
and as we proceed,
I think you'll glean.

You're a dead man,
let it be known.
You've been bought by blood.
You're not your own.

So when words of anger,
come your way,
it doesn't bother you,
what they say.

When emotions stir,
and you want to be violent,
just shed them off,
and remain silent.

If unforgiveness shows,
just give it a nudge,
and let it know,
you won't hold a grudge.

You're a dead man,
and do not pout.
Your tongue is controlled,
and doesn't lash out.

Now here's the point,
of what I said.
Be led of the Spirit,
and of the flesh be dead.

Your life will show,
as you do these things,
great strides forward,
and improved change.

APRIL 16

CARNAL MIND

Man has five senses,
to help him to live.
Each has its part,
with something to give.

They're all important,
when properly used,
but from the eye of the spirit,
they can often abuse.

The carnal mind is ruled,
by all of them,
affecting God's light,
and making it dim.

God's Word often differs,
from perceptions of flesh.
Opposing each other,
they don't often mesh.

When this takes place,
it should be understood,
that the Word takes priority,
and always should.

The five senses are great,
it must be said,
but monitor your spirit,
to be properly led.

The candle of the Lord,
shines light to your inner man,
giving him direction,
and helping him stand.

The Word and the Spirit,
will be as one.
They'll be in agreement.
Consider it done.

So don't drop guard,
against the carnal mind,
by ignoring God's Word,
and becoming spiritually blind.

Again I proclaim,
to be perfectly clear,
be spiritually minded,
and look through God's mirror.

APRIL 17

ATMOSPHERE

Breathe that smoke,
in that room.
Hanging in the air,
it heavily looms.

In that traffic,
breathe those fumes.
At the stop light,
it heavily looms.

Near that factory,
smell that pollution.
I'm sure you'll agree,
it needs resolution.

The air you breathe,
it has an affect,
on your health,
so don't neglect.

As the atmosphere you breathe,
affects your physical side,
it's the same spiritually,
and cannot be denied.

How and where you spend your time,
will have a direct affect,
on your spiritual growth.
You'll feel the affects.

Your eyes and ears,
are vessels of use,
but they can become instruments,
for spiritual abuse.

The atmosphere is important.
Make no mistake,
don't take it for granted,
for your spiritual sake.

APRIL 18

FALSELY ACCUSED

Many people believe,
that suffering for Christ,
is very noble,
and almost nice.

Let's take a look,
at some of these beliefs,
to determine truth,
and get some relief.

Many people believe,
that sickness is of God,
but when I search the scriptures,
I find that odd.

Many people believe,
that poverty is of God,
but when I search the scriptures,
I find that equally odd.

Many people believe,
that when disaster strikes lives,
that it was sent from God,
when many don't survive.

So many times,
God is falsely accused,
while the devil must smile,
and become very amused.

The thief comes,
to steal, kill and destroy,
so let's be frank,
and not be coy.

God is a good god,
while Satan is a bad devil,
don't confuse the two,
for Satan does the evil.

Suffering for Christ,
means to deny the flesh,
not allowing its way,
the scriptures attest.

Another rose for God's garden,
not really so.
It wasn't God's doing,
you should know.

APRIL 19

EVIDENCE

The gavel goes down,
as the court session begins.
The people stand up,
as the judge enters in.

The trial commences,
before all in the court.
As the jury looks on,
the truth it must sort.

The jury will listen,
as the evidence is weighed.
It will all be considered,
before the verdict is made.

You're the one on trial,
or didn't you know?
You'll either be convicted,
or set free to go.

The court will determine,
if you're a Christian or not,
by examining the evidence,
going through the whole lot.

Did you witness for Jesus,
and share the gospel,
or did you remain silent,
and to no one tell?

Were good works done,
in the Lord's Name,
or did you often cuss,
using it in vain?

Was the love of God,
in your life seen,
or were you to people,
both selfish and mean?

Would people say,
if they were asked,
that you're a Christian,
with their vote cast?

The evidence is in,
what will it be?
The way you live,
provides the key.

APRIL 20

EYE OF THE EAGLE

The eye of the eagle,
has great sight.
It can spot its prey,
while in flight.

At great distance it sees,
with remarkable clarity,
spotting the slightest of movements,
with amazing accuracy.

The eye is sharp,
for defense as well,
protecting the eagle,
where it dwells.

As the eye helps the eagle,
so the Holy Spirit helps you,
to lead and guide you,
in all you do.

He knows God's plan,
for your years,
and will speak to your spirit,
if you'll hear.

The Holy Spirit sees ahead,
down your life's road.
He knows where the curves are,
and where you'll pull heavy loads.

He'll help you to know,
when to take the offensive.
Spotting traps of the devil,
He'll help you with defenses.

The eye of the Holy Spirit,
is sharp indeed.
He'll keep you from mistakes,
if His advice you'll heed.

He knows what's best,
and will steer you right,
throughout all your years,
both day and night.

A friend He'll be,
if you'll be led.
With the eye of the eagle,
He'll look ahead.

APRIL 21

WHAT ARE YOU LOOKING AT?

Two realms exist,
they can be defined as seen and unseen.
Things seen are temporal.
Things not seen are eternal.

Too many Christians,
after they pray,
lose track of this.
You can tell by what they say.

After a sincere prayer,
they continue to look at the circumstances.
They look for immediate change,
that may involve an unsaved loved one or
possibly finances.

Spiritual forces were released,
but these focused reactions aren't good.
They're supposed to walk in faith,
like the Bible tells them they should.

Being moved by circumstances,
will cause Christians to waver.
It'll affect their prayers,
and of results will sever.

The Just are to live by faith,
and focus on the spiritual realm.
Trust God in your prayers,
and expect God to honor them.

Things in the temporal,
are subject to change.
Believe God is at work,
to bring favorable things.

What are you looking at?
Are you wavering and looking at things seen,
or are you trusting God,
knowing that He's working in the unseen?

APRIL 22

ICEBERG

It floats as ice,
out in the sea,
with only its tip,
for people to see.

Below the surface,
is its base.
It's like that in churches,
the same kind of case.

The pastor preaches,
from the pulpit,
as the church looks on,
from where they sit.

Their eyes are on him,
as he gets their attention,
but there's so much more,
that I must mention.

Much work was done,
before the service,
to keep the pastor,
from getting nervous.

The majority can't see,
all the work that was done,
so people could hear,
all about God's Son.

The ministry of helps,
was in effect,
to get the church ready,
without slightest neglect.

A spirit of excellence,
is easily perceived,
around the sanctuary,
so others could receive.

Others have worked,
performing diligent deeds,
to enable the pastor,
to take his lead.

So the next time you go,
to hear the Word,
as you look at the pastor,
remember the iceberg.

APRIL 23

SAND CASTLES

Sand castles are built,
from sand on the beach,
up near the berm,
out of tidal reach.

Much care is used,
to build them fine.
Using much effort,
some take time.

Then a storm shows up,
pushing the waves up high,
washing down the sand castles,
now no longer dry.

The storm came.
They didn't stand,
not built real strong,
but made of sand.

Sand castles are built,
in many peoples' hearts.
Not grounded in the Word,
they'll fall apart.

These sand castles are made,
from materials of carnality.
Built with defects,
they lack true spirituality.

When life's pressures come,
and the winds do blow,
the walls will weaken,
and down they'll go.

Foundations weren't built,
with the Word in heart,
of quality materials,
that won't fall apart.

The Word will sustain you,
as you weather the test.
Put it in your heart,
and you'll surely be blessed.

Forget all the sand,
and build your house strong.
Put the Word in your heart,
and you won't go wrong.

APRIL 24

METAMORPHOSIS

A caterpillar is fuzzy,
before taking a cocoon,
but a metamorphosis will come,
that will happen soon.

His new home is woven,
as he nestles in,
surrounded by a shell,
that creates his den.

The change begins,
from view of man's eyes,
as his shape becomes different,
and so does his size.

The cocoon opens,
and a butterfly shows,
displaying beautiful colors,
as he dramatically goes.

Departing the cocoon,
he suddenly takes flight,
such a remarkable change,
such a beautiful sight.

One begins to think,
of the new birth.
It's the greatest change,
of all on earth.

Colors are beautiful,
but so is white,
when sins are washed away,
before God's sight.

It's a spiritual event,
that's of the highest rate,
sparking the host of Heaven,
to joyfully celebrate.

The sinner comes to God,
redeemed by the Lamb,
his spirit reborn,
when once it was damned.

A miracle it is,
second to none,
an instantaneous change,
when one accepts God's Son.

APRIL 25

RUSTY OLD SPIKES

Let's discuss rusty old spikes,
if you will,
as they relate to Calvary,
at Jerusalem's hill.

Great pain to Christ,
the opposite of bliss,
how they were used,
to provide salvation's kiss.

They were used,
to free all generations,
from Satan's grasp,
and all his oppression.

A seed was sown,
by God that day,
death for Christ,
in earth He lay.

But a harvest was grown,
from earth's clay,
as Christ did rise,
on Resurrection day.

Sons and daughters were saved,
their names now on Father's list,
brought into the Kingdom,
to experience Heaven's bliss.

Figure this out,
don't even try.
Just accept God's love,
and then you'll know why.

Rusty old spikes,
items of Satan's use,
helped break the shackles,
to set you loose.

APRIL 26

GO GET A DONKEY

Go get a donkey,
is what Jesus said,
to His disciples,
as He was led.

Going to Jerusalem,
He had a need,
as His disciples,
completed the deed.

Today it's not different,
than way back when,
when Jesus had a need,
not changing since then.

The gospel must be sent,
all across the land,
and a key part is played,
by the born again man.

His voice is used,
and plays a key role,
but so does his resources,
to reach men's souls.

Tithes and offerings are used,
to send forth God's work.
The needs are real,
and cannot be shirked.

The Master speaks,
and the good steward comes near,
to carry out His directions,
and all that he hears.

Go get a donkey,
will you obey,
as Jesus calls out,
to you today?

APRIL 27

FIRE STARTER

The fire doesn't start,
if there's no wood.
So watch your words,
as you know you should.

Watch the gossip,
with words of haste,
for they sow discord,
and bring distaste.

Words of slander,
bite real deep,
against the recipient,
they're not real neat.

Release arrogant words,
against a life,
and they'll often generate,
fighting and strife.

Fires are fueled,
by the tongue,
creating havoc,
that rates with dung.

Without fuel,
the fire goes out.
So watch your words,
from your mouth.

From your words,
harm can come.
So speak well,
or remain mum.

Monitor your tongue,
does it edify?
If it hurts others,
then you must mortify.

APRIL 28

FOG

Fog rolls in,
low to the ground.
With feline movement,
it doesn't make a sound.

Before you know it,
it's suddenly there,
obscuring your vision,
as you look into the air.

Squint as you may,
its presence is real.
The fog has set in,
presenting its seal.

The things of the world,
will do the same,
not known as fog,
but using other names.

Worldly television,
will begin to taint,
and affect the walk,
of the godly saint.

Worldly friendships,
will affect as well.
Better watch yourself,
for worldly sells.

No time for worship,
or even praise,
better reevaluate your time,
during your day.

Schedule too busy,
with too much care,
better watch yourself,
when you drop prayer.

These things creep in,
and before you know,
you've noticed you've slipped,
to a spiritual low.

Worldly matters entice,
and are so real,
to fog your walk,
so refuse its deal.

APRIL 29

TREASURE MAP

The treasure map reveals,
where treasure is buried,
causing its seekers,
to run and scurry.

Get the map,
is what they seek,
to find the mark,
and take a peek.

Once they find it,
they'll start to dig,
looking for the chest,
and something big.

Don't look elsewhere,
there's now no need.
You know the mark,
and where it leads.

It's really like that,
with the Bible,
as you find the truth,
and become a disciple.

You've found the mark,
so start to dig,
with each chapter,
there's something big.

You've found the truth,
in this book,
so forget the others,
no need to look.

There's reason to celebrate,
and rejoice with glee,
for you've found great treasure,
and have been set free.

APRIL 30

INVESTIGATIVE REPORT

Let's take a look,
and gather our information,
so we can better conduct,
a thorough investigation.

Once we have it,
we can figure out,
and provide some answers,
to some honest doubt.

On the cross,
Christ did die,
but before He went,
He said He would rise.

The disciples did flee,
afraid for their lives,
after Christ was crucified,
they sought to survive.

But on the third day,
a strange event occurred,
when Mary Magdalene,
heard the Master's words.

Go tell my disciples,
Christ did say,
that I have risen,
this very day.

Peter and John heard,
and ran to the tomb,
and saw it empty,
as they entered the room.

What matter is this,
they seriously pondered.
It made an impression,
and made them wonder.

So in a room,
where the disciples gathered,
Christ appeared,
to settle the matter.

The disciples changed,
and renewed their course,
with great determination,
and no remorse.

MAY 1

NOT AN AUTOMATON

Programmed to work,
in a regimented way,
the automaton moves,
with a mechanical sway.

Guided to follow,
a channeled path,
there isn't latitude,
for wiring that's cast.

Freedom of choice,
cannot be made.
It isn't an option,
in the blueprint laid.

So let us look,
at the human man,
and discuss a difference,
if we can.

God gave man choice,
it's what He sought.
A wonderful work,
that God did wrought.

Fellowship was desired,
but it must be by choice,
that man would choose God,
making His heart rejoice.

God won't force Himself,
onto His created man.
It's man's personal choice,
a part of God's wonderful plan.

The power of choice,
is clearly a free gift.
For those that don't want God,
it will certainly sift.

The Father calls out,
to each man's ears.
Accept His invitation,
for eternal years.

An automaton man's not,
for he can choose,
salvation to gain,
or his soul to lose.

MAY 2

THE CHAMELEON

The chameleon changes color,
of his skin,
adjusting to his environment,
to blend in.

From area to area,
he moves around,
sometimes quietly,
without making a sound.

He makes you think,
of some Christians,
who seem to have forgotten,
the great commission.

The gospel isn't shared,
so not to offend.
They just don't share it,
and try to blend in.

Are they ashamed,
of the gospel story,
or maybe embarrassed,
and prone to worry?

Are carnal friends,
on a higher scale,
than pleasing God,
and delivering His mail?

You're in the world,
but not of it,
so shine your light,
and keep it lit.

Don't hide it away,
under a cover,
for others must see,
or they may suffer.

Live for God,
in both word and deed,
and into lives,
you'll plant good seed.

Others will take notice,
as you shine for Him,
for they need the Lord,
and His blessings for them.

MAY 3

THIS LION HAS NO TEETH

The devil comes,
as a roaring lion,
making lots of noise,
looking for fearful signs.

Keep the Christian,
in the dark,
and the roar will scare him,
off his mark.

From the Lord,
authority is given,
to the Christian,
it's backed by Heaven.

The devil flees,
as in terror,
when authority is executed,
no matter what hour.

So the devil tries,
to shield this fact,
from the Christian,
to keep him in lack.

If the Christian looked,
into the lion's jaw,
he would notice no teeth,
nonc at all.

They were pulled,
many years ago,
but the devil doesn't want,
the Christian to know.

The devil was conquered,
at the cross,
when Jesus died,
to save the lost.

But authority came,
with this deal,
when Christians accepted,
salvation's seal.

So know the devil,
cannot bite,
just use your authority,
and put him to flight.

MAY 4

RADIO STATION

Radio signals are sent,
from a tower tall,
throughout the area,
that can be received by all.

If the dial is set,
to the right station,
then the frequency comes in,
to that part of the nation.

Power is important,
to cover more turf,
but I know of a source,
that covers the whole earth.

His name is Holy Spirit,
and signals He sends,
to accept Jesus as Lord,
and to repent of all sins.

He sends to all hearts,
and His message is clear,
but tuning is required,
in order to hear.

Some people could receive,
but refuse to listen,
determining in their hearts,
not to become Christians.

On the other hand,
others will receive,
and listen intently,
and choose to believe.

The signals go forth,
from the same station,
available for all,
throughout all nations.

All have a radio,
it's their spirit.
For you see,
they were born with it.

So on Judgment Day,
when many didn't repent,
they won't be able to say,
that the signals weren't sent.

MAY 5

UPSTREAM SWIM

Against strong currents,
some fish do swim,
traveling great distances,
many miles for them.

Perseverance is required,
to swim upstream.
It's not an easy task,
but a demanding scene.

The easier course says,
to swim with the flow,
but the fish refuse,
and upstream they go.

Christians face choices,
in a similar vein,
to swim upstream,
or remain the same.

They pray in faith,
but now must stand.
Perseverance is required,
to possess the land.

Stand on the promises,
don't let go.
Swim upstream,
against the flow.

Circumstances speak loud,
but so does God's Word.
Give it priority,
the promises you've heard.

Currents of doubt,
may toward you veer,
but remain strong,
and do not fear.

Set your heart,
as cast in mint.
Refuse to compromise,
with eyes of flint.

As time does pass,
look for your prize.
You know that you know,
it will surely arrive.

MAY 6

YOU REAP WHAT YOU SOW

A spiritual law exists,
that affects us all,
no matter who you are,
both great or small.

This I'll say,
you reap what you sow.
Consider it awhile,
and then you'll know.

You reap what you sow,
it's really true.
So be conscious of this,
in all you do.

Whatever you sow,
it will come in return.
You can plan on it.
Consider it done.

Some may think,
they can beat this law,
but that's not so,
it applies to all.

So live your life,
in this light.
Consider your deeds,
and make them right.

Sow good seed,
and begin to reap,
or sow bad seed,
and feel the heat.

The choice is yours,
that you must make.
So sow good seed,
for your own sake.

MAY 7

THE MIDNIGHT HOUR

Adversity will come,
and trials will knock.
Standing at your door,
they will mock.

No one is immune,
from their faces,
for they'll show up,
in all sorts of places.

Even at midnight,
adversity may call,
when a trial comes,
like to Silas and Paul.

At Philippi they were chained,
in a cold and dark prison,
for preaching the gospel,
which was the only reason.

The situation wasn't good,
and hope appeared bleak,
when Paul and Silas,
began to speak.

They sang unto God,
with voices of praise,
gaining the victory,
from defeat they were raised.

The shackles came loose,
and the earth did shake,
setting them free,
at their cell's gate.

When your midnight hour comes,
remember this story.
Begin to praise God,
and give Him glory.

You're not thanking Him,
for the sorrow or pain,
but for the deliverance,
that you're about to gain.

So praise His Name,
and when you do,
He'll be there with you,
to pull you through.

MAY 8

THE BEST ROBE

Let's celebrate,
and kill the fatted calf.
Prepare the feast,
and let's all laugh.

The son has come home,
after time astray.
He has come to his senses,
on this glorious day.

Once he was lost,
but now he's home,
back with his father,
no more to roam.

Get the best robe,
let's make haste.
Put it on him,
no time to waste.

It's an interesting story,
the prodigal son,
but look at it spiritually,
to see what was done.

The son is lost,
out selling his soul.
A story so common,
it doesn't grow old.

He's convicted of his sins,
and knows he has done wrong,
so he seeks forgiveness,
for which he now longs.

To the altar he goes,
to set things right,
as the Father awaits him,
and keeps him in sight.

The Father is pleased,
to say the least,
for He always loved him,
it never ceased.

There is joy in Heaven,
over a saved soul.
A story so fresh,
it never grows old.

MAY 9

THE REAL CULPRIT

When people do wrong,
and to you afflict,
remember this truth,
and do not neglect.

When harsh words are said,
to make you upset,
remember this truth,
and do not neglect.

The devil's at work,
behind the scenes,
influencing people,
to act real mean.

He has strategies,
to throw at you.
They're well designed,
to make you blue.

He wants your peace,
and people he'll use,
in well planned schemes,
to make you blue.

So at flesh and blood,
don't get mad.
Remember the source,
and don't get sad.

Put a smile on your face,
and attack the devil,
using God's Word,
to bind his evil.

God's Word will work.
It's guaranteed,
to bring victory,
against Satan's deeds.

Put joy in your heart,
and rise up strong.
Resist his plans,
with all their wrong.

He'll quickly know,
as he flees from you,
that you're wise to him,
and his plans of blue.

MAY 10

DIVINE PAIN

Come with me,
and take a look,
into a story,
from the good Book.

On the Mount of Olives,
in the Garden of Gethsemane,
you'll observe this story,
and perceive the agony.

Jesus is deep in prayer,
and about to go to the cross,
to take man's sin,
and die for the lost.

To be separated from the Father,
and his great love,
was not an easy task,
that was ordained from above.

Pain for the Father,
and pain for the Son,
it's hard for humans,
to perceive what was done.

You can be sure,
that pain was there,
but Jesus would endure,
and this task would bare.

Angels stood silent,
and keenly observed,
the impending torment,
that Christ didn't deserve.

Puzzled they were,
as they watched this scene unfold,
but they knew the Father was at work,
and would do as were told.

It wasn't easy for Jesus,
for real was this pain,
that demonstrated God's love,
and conquered man's shame.

Jesus had trust in His Father,
and His salvation plan,
and would take this pain,
in order to save man.

MAY 11

YOUR HOUSE IS BURNING

"Your house is burning!"
so says the neighbor.
It's whether clear,
it's a moment not savored.

Reaction was quick,
the fire was put out,
and all because,
of the good neighbor's shout.

Check your neighborhood,
and prepare to shout,
when you spot fires,
that need to be put out.

They'll be there,
and will be easy to tell,
for the road is wide,
so prepare to yell.

People are coasting,
from day-to-day,
with one foot in Hell,
and the other on way.

They haven't received the truth,
it's blinded from their sight.
So they need to hear God's message,
before it becomes their final night.

Speak out boldly,
and help them learn,
that their house is on fire,
and has commenced to burn.

Water that fire,
and kill the flame.
Don't remain silent,
and be partially to blame.

Shame on them,
if they choose to ignore.
At least it was them,
that closed their doors.

But praise be to God,
if they choose to receive,
after hearing the gospel,
and choose to believe.

MAY 12

LINE UPON LINE

Line upon line,
precept upon precept,
that's how you learn,
in this biblical concept.

Get good teaching,
and listen to the Word.
Meditate on it,
and what you heard.

Study a little there.
Study a little here.
Listen to some good tapes,
and keep them near.

As time goes by,
deposits are made,
building on the foundation,
that with salvation was laid.

Growth takes place,
as knowledge has increased,
but continue to study,
and it will not cease.

Line upon line,
that's how it's done,
when your walk started,
after accepting God's Son.

MAY 13

ABOUT FACE

Military drills exist,
to train the men.
Each movement has a purpose,
to get them to blend.

Discipline is taught,
with each march.
A unit is molded,
as a shirt with starch.

One command does bring,
the gospel to mind,
as the troops react,
and corroborate with sign.

"About face!",
the command is barked,
as the troops turn around,
and to those words hark.

It's like that with sin,
when told to repent,
a choice is made,
to choose to relent.

"Repent!" is a command,
its message is clear,
to turn from sin,
and its items dear.

Turn completely around,
as you respond to correction,
and set your eyes on,
your new direction.

You've made your decision.
You're part of God's unit.
So get in place,
and get on with it.

MAY 14

STADIUM CROWD

The crowd is gathered,
to cheer their team.
There's lots of yelling,
and smiles that beam.

A football is used,
that's made of pigskin.
It's pumped with air,
between its two ends.

The football is pushed,
up and down the field,
as the defense seeks it,
and attempts to steal.

With great excitement,
the people react,
when the home team scores,
or gets a sack.

People will cheer,
over this simple game,
but to cheer for Jesus,
it's not the same.

People don't realize,
it's totally absurd,
to refuse Jesus,
and not accept His Word.

Over a meaningless game,
they will wildly cheer,
as they greatly enjoy,
their cups of beer.

Not few but many,
these games will be,
the greatest excitement,
they'll ever see.

They cheer for a bag of air,
moving all around,
and yell real loud,
amidst all the sounds.

It's really sad,
for there's so much more,
but they'll never see it,
or broach Heaven's door.

MAY 15

AN ASTRONAUT'S VIEW

The spaceship sits,
not making a sound,
but soon it'll be prepared,
to leave earth's ground.

The engines are started,
creating much sound.
It's ready to blast off,
and noise does abound.

High it goes,
past earth's clouds.
The higher it goes,
it becomes less loud.

It's almost out of sight,
from man's eyes,
appearing much smaller,
becoming less in size.

The astronaut's view,
of earth has changed.
As he looks from space,
it appears to just hang.

A different perspective,
he now perceives,
an eternal image,
that will never leave.

Earth is surrounded,
by miles of space,
making him refocus,
on God's great grace.

Life is short,
but there's a another dimension,
much like the astronaut's view,
that I must mention.

Life doesn't stop,
after earthly years.
The spirit lives forever,
so now please hear.

There's something greater,
this side of earth,
and it all begins,
with the new birth.

MAY 16

CLOUDS

Different shapes and sizes,
are easily seen,
when one looks upwards,
towards the skyward scene.

Clouds paint the sky,
moving to and fro,
with a slight wind,
they move real slow.

Increase the breeze,
and faster they go.
You'll clearly see,
they're no longer slow.

Sometimes they're fluffy,
cumulus by name,
or perhaps shaped differently,
under a different name.

In a nice blue sky,
they'll appear bright,
but in a thunderstorm,
they'll often fright.

The sky will change,
as peoples' moods shift,
causing the weathermen,
to be often miffed.

Parallels exist,
between clouds and men.
It's easy to see,
they're formed from God's hand.

Sometimes try to imagine,
and if you can,
you'll see some with faces,
in the design of man.

MAY 17

ROADBLOCKS

Roadblocks block the road,
to halt vehicles on the move.
They're clearly designed,
to keep them from going through.

Up they go,
to block the road.
With just their presence,
they'll stop heavy loads.

Roadblocks are also used,
in the spiritual realm,
to come against Christians,
all of them.

The devil is a master,
of disguise,
and cloaks himself,
with many lies.

He'll try to affect,
a person's life,
and bring into it,
both arguing and strife.

Sickness is used,
in his bag of tricks,
thrown against you,
in an attempt to lick.

These roadblocks are real,
but so is God's grace.
So stand on the Word,
throughout all your race.

Authority is yours,
it was given by the Lord.
So get in the Word,
and wield its sword.

Keep your car rolling,
no need to stop.
You may be a bit slowed,
but defeated you're not.

You're going through,
you have passage ahead.
You're standing on God's Word,
for you believe what He said.

MAY 18

CREATION

Open your eyes,
that you may see,
all the creation,
set before thee.

Order exists,
it greatly abounds.
Take another look,
look all around.

Checks and balances,
they all exist.
Look again,
and please don't miss.

Planets are set,
hung in space,
held by physical laws,
each in place.

Look at science,
and consider biology,
and how it's supported,
by earth's ecology.

Man creates items,
from his intelligent mind,
with system and order,
they serve as signs.

There's rhyme and reason,
to each complex invention,
developed from the human mind,
with a series of systems.

Everything about life,
has a definitive order.
Now let's think about this,
and for a moment loiter.

Can this kind of order,
from chaos come?
Take a closer look,
and don't be dumb.

An intelligent being,
put this in place.
His name is God,
and this ends my case.

MAY 19

TREADING WATER

When a swimmer treads water,
he remains in place.
Keeping his head above water,
he keeps his pace.

It's different from strokes,
when much distance is gained,
for the swimmer stays stationary,
while treading in lane.

You're going somewhere,
when you use strokes,
even if you swim slowly,
like a slow poke.

But when water is tread,
no distance is gained,
although effort is made,
while kicking in lane.

It's like that for Christians,
or so it seems,
but always remember,
you've been redeemed.

God has a plan,
for your life.
Your clay is being shaped,
under a sculptor's knife.

Deposits are being made,
during life's journey,
even during slow periods,
both cloudy and sunny.

Timing is important,
and God knows this.
So don't get too anxious,
or you just might miss.

Things are being arranged,
for God is at work.
Trust in His schedule,
and avoid much hurt.

You're going somewhere,
for God has a plan.
So remain patient in Him,
and trust in His hand.

MAY 20

BATTLEGROUND

Scenes are set,
on earth's battlegrounds.
It's where adversaries meet,
and are easily found.

Planes will attack,
and launch their bombs,
where explosions take place,
and dispenses of calm.

Artillery reacts,
and aims on high,
shooting at planes,
cruising the sky.

Tanks roll in,
making menacing sounds,
seeking the enemy,
while grinding the ground.

Some soldiers live,
and some soldiers die.
It happens in war,
no need to lie.

Look closer at home,
for your own personal war.
It takes place in your mind,
when you open its door.

Thoughts are tossed,
to make you think,
opposite of God's Word,
to make you sink.

Meditate on them,
and it will cost,
often most dearly,
with battles lost.

It's the major tool,
used by the devil,
aimed at your mind,
to perpetrate evil.

The battleground is set.
It's in your mind,
so don't listen to the devil,
or give him your time.

MAY 21

ATTITUDE

Approach to a task,
can be a good thermometer.
If pressure builds,
check your barometer.

Attitude is important,
in our approach to life,
a poor one often leads,
to friction and strife.

A poor attitude within,
can rob you blind,
creating discontent,
it's a warning sign.

A good attitude within,
on the other side,
makes things easier,
nothing to hide.

Life goes on,
with a choice to make.
Have a good attitude,
for your own sake.

A task can be done,
with a good or bad attitude,
but in the things of God,
it will affect your altitude.

MAY 22

HOURGLASS

The sand is sifting,
through the hourglass of time.
It just keeps moving,
this sand so fine.

Years keep passing,
one by one,
as nights keep passing,
with the rising sun.

Not much sand left,
it now appears.
As it keeps on moving,
it'll soon disappear.

Know for sure,
a lesson is here.
The Lord is coming,
and His arrival is near.

The hourglass of time,
is about to run out.
Look at the signs around you,
and have no doubt.

Better wake up,
no time to sleep.
Missing the Lord,
would not be neat.

You may not know the day,
but you'll know the season.
So I appeal to you,
and your ability to reason.

Open your eyes,
the signs are there.
Don't miss this meeting,
in earth's air.

MAY 23

TRUTH VERSUS SINCERITY

Sincerity is nice,
in its own way,
but truth is more important,
listen to what I say.

Sincere mistakes have been made,
throughout all of time.
They're often very severe,
and not of simple kind.

Look in the Book of Mark,
and turn to the last chapter.
It's towards the end,
that I want you to capture.

Go forth and preach the gospel,
it clearly states,
that this is the way of salvation,
make no mistake.

He who believeth would be saved,
and he who believeth not would be damned.
You'll notice that salvation,
is through the blood of the Lamb.

No other name is written,
so please take heed.
Come to the Lord Jesus,
it's Him you need.

Truth is more important,
I will attest.
So don't miss Jesus,
or you'll be in a mess.

No other name,
under the sun,
leads to salvation,
but God's only Son.

It's time to turn,
from whom you serve.
So look to Jesus,
and to Him do swerve.

Leave false doctrines,
and to Jesus grasp,
for eternal life,
and to be set free at last.

MAY 24

RECEIVE HIS MAIL

My heart just told me,
that he received a letter today.
It came from someone special,
and had nice words to say.

Paper was not used,
nor in envelope enclosed.
It didn't arrive by normal way,
as you might suppose.

Words were not written,
but they were clear,
spoken with much love,
that I now hold dear.

Imprinted in my heart,
they will ever be,
words of encouragement,
that were meant for me.

I know from where they came,
for I know His voice.
They came from my Master.
I accepted Him by choice.

I'm so glad,
and thus I'll mention,
that when I accepted Him,
it was my wisest decision.

He communicates with me,
on a regular routine,
always trying to help,
and He never is mean.

Just come to Jesus.
You'll think Him swell.
Stamps are not needed,
to receive His mail.

His letters are delivered,
to one's heart's place.
They're always good for you,
and coated with grace.

His letters are great,
and to you I'll tell,
accept Him as Lord,
and receive His mail.

MAY 25

SAM GOT HIS GUN

Three people died,
just last night.
On the rug they fell,
creating a gruesome sight.

Two murdered and a suicide,
the report does say.
The deeds have been done,
can't reverse the day.

Sam argued with Mary,
and became very distraught,
over their breakup,
and relationship fraught.

Furious he left,
to get his gun,
to return later at night,
where the crime was to be done.

Mary was nervous,
and needed an ear,
so she sought Peter out,
to listen and hear.

Over he came,
to sit in her room,
attempting to console,
before the gloom.

Sam came back,
and knocked on the door.
As Peter answered,
he fell to the floor.

Sam had shot him,
upon seeing his face,
and proceeded to shoot Mary,
in a fit of disgrace.

He then shot himself,
to complete this act,
of which the evidence supports,
and does not lack.

But let's look deeper,
behind the scene,
and you'll see demons at work,
in a strategical scheme.

MAY 26

THE SPONGE

Designed to absorb,
the sponge is a useful tool.
This is easy to observe,
there's no need of school.

Observe as you will,
observe as you may,
it absorbs up liquid,
what more to say.

Eyes and ears,
I will next address,
and depending on how they're used,
will lead to success or mess.

Your heart is a sponge,
that uses your eyes and ears.
It absorbs information,
from what you see and hear.

Liquid is liquid,
and information is information,
as absorption is made,
there effects a transformation.

The sponge becomes full,
and so does your heart,
on what it absorbed,
throughout all its parts.

Squeeze the sponge,
and you'll know what's there.
Now look into your heart,
if you dare.

Let's not pretend,
influences are real.
They come with life,
it's part of earth's deal.

Guard your eyes,
and guard ears,
on what you see,
and what you hear.

This is very important,
some sound advice.
Don't discard this lightly,
it will help your life.

<u>MAY 27</u>

INSTRUCTION MANUAL

To build an item,
you look at the instructions,
to make it work right,
through quality construction.

Follow the guidelines,
when details are given.
It's important to maintain,
your quality precision.

Pay close attention,
and avoid distractions.
The result will be,
one of satisfaction.

An instruction manual exists,
for all of man's life.
Decisions can be made,
without rolling dice.

Wisdom will be found,
throughout all its pages.
It was clearly written,
for all the ages.

Follow its guidance,
and you will be,
the wiser man,
just wait and see.

Successful living,
it will prescribe.
I guarantee you,
I haven't lied.

This manual is available,
to one and all,
to rich or poor,
or short or tall.

So take my advice,
and take the lead,
by opening its cover,
and begin to read.

It's the treasured Bible,
of which I speak.
Begin with the gospel,
and of wisdom seek.

<u>MAY 28</u>

THE CHURCH

Build the church,
with a tall steeple.
Make it look nice,
for all the people.

Get good pews,
and place them in rows,
and allow aisle space,
for easy flow.

Get excellent carpet,
and pick a nice color.
Check for value,
against the dollar.

Stain glass windows,
sure are fine,
and don't forget to advertise,
with church signs.

Parking is important,
so plan lot space.
Use the area wisely,
and do not waste.

These things are good,
but let's take pause,
and consider these thoughts,
with good cause.

A building is important,
but a church it's not.
It just provides a meeting place,
on a section of lot.

Now here's the point.
The church is the people.
It has nothing to do,
with high steeples.

A nice setting is good,
it enhances praise,
but here's the point,
that I will raise.

Keep people as focus,
as you fill each seat.
Keep them your priority,
it's the reason you meet.

MAY 29

BOW AND ARROW

Pick up the arrow,
and place it on the bow.
Now set your sight,
before you let it go.

Hold it firmly,
and pull the string.
Let it go quickly,
after taking aim.

You hit your target.
You were right on mark.
Your words hurt deeply,
as you hit the heart.

Pain was felt,
more than you know,
as words were sent,
from your mouth's bow.

Bitter they were,
and coarse indeed,
as they planted,
some hateful seed.

Words can be weapons,
and cause serious hurt.
So keep your guard up,
and remain on alert.

Watch what you say,
and maintain your peace,
for you can't take back,
what you've just released.

If the button is pushed,
and missile sent high,
it's then too late,
to retrieve from sky.

MAY 30

ACORNS

The squirrel is gathering acorns,
near that oak tree,
busily he works,
what a sight to see.

Storage is in order,
it's part of his plan,
even as eyes look on,
from those of man.

Winter is coming,
brisk is the air.
Storage is a must,
so better prepare.

Survive he will,
because he planned,
by gathering acorns,
from the autumn land.

Now open your eyes,
and observe his deeds,
then take action,
and follow his lead.

Plan ahead,
and prepare yourself.
Get on the train,
and don't get left.

Work is required,
it'll be worthwhile,
as fruits will come,
so hold that dial.

Be steadfast,
and stay a diligent man.
Summer will come,
and you'll walk in its sand.

MAY 31

THE MOST BEAUTIFUL SITE

The painted desert,
provides a beautiful site,
as do many stars,
on a very clear night.

The Grand Canyon,
yields a spectacular view,
as does a valley green,
covered with dew.

Niagara Falls,
certainly makes the list,
of beautiful scenes,
sealed by nature's kiss.

Mt. Rainier,
majestic in peak,
projects an image,
that photographers seek.

National forests,
preserved so well,
portray nature's beauty,
as visitors will tell.

The mighty rivers
woven into the land,
are greatly appreciated,
by the eyes of man.

Yet, all these sites,
added into one,
do not match,
the acceptance of God's Son.

The most beautiful sight,
to the Father's eyes,
is a sinner snatched,
from the devil's lies.

The new birth,
is a grand event,
that saves a man,
from being Hell sent.

Rejoicing occurs,
in Heaven above,
when one accepts Jesus,
and God's sweet love.

JUNE 1

LIFT AND THRUST

I got on an airplane today.
We departed the gate,
and proceeded on time,
and avoided being late.

As we departed the ground,
then I saw,
houses appearing smaller,
and perceived a physical law.

Up, up we went,
into the sky,
and it wasn't long,
until we were very high.

Gravity pulled,
but it was overcome,
by a greater law,
to which it had to succumb.

Lift and thrust,
exerted its force,
lifting the airplane,
to get it on course.

Laws exist,
in the spiritual realm,
that can affect adverse situations,
overpowering them.

Do not discount,
the words I speak,
if it is truth,
that you do seek.

God's Word has power.
So now please learn,
that it's available for all,
if we'll just discern.

Circumstances can change,
when the Word is used.
It's backed by God,
so you just can't lose.

God's Word is truth,
I will endorse.
So know and do it,
and change your course.

JUNE 2

TRAGEDY

The ambulance left,
in a state of urgency.
It has just departed,
for a critical emergency.

Quickly it goes,
for time is short,
to answer in time,
the life threatening report.

The driver makes haste,
and with siren sounds,
as his wheels turn quickly,
covering much ground.

Assistance is required,
as their wits are keen,
to render first aid,
at the accident's scene.

The accident reveals,
an atheist hurt.
Blood can be seen,
on his clean white shirt.

Will they make it,
the man asks himself?
For he clearly senses,
he has only minutes left.

His last breath going,
he lets out a sigh,
for he now knows,
he's about to die.

The ambulance was late,
and so it seems,
for it didn't show,
quick enough on scene.

But the real tragedy is this,
it's crystal clear.
The man refused Christ,
and His blood so dear.

Eternity will be spent,
in Hell's abyss,
another deceived,
now on Satan's list.

JUNE 3

REST IN THE STORM

A storm came up,
in the midst of the sea.
The boat did rock,
causing bracing of knees.

The wind did blow,
throughout the air,
affecting the waves,
and everyone there.

The waves pushed up,
creating a sight,
that caused great attention,
and generated fright.

The disciples yelled,
to get Jesus' attention.
They were quite concerned,
over the sea's condition.

Jesus spoke to the storm,
after he did rise,
and calmed the seas,
and the windy sky.

Asleep Jesus was,
the King of Kings,
during the storm,
what could this mean?

What can be learned,
from this story,
when we are prone,
to fret and worry?

Trust in the Word,
and rest in the Lord,
remain calm in the storm,
and receive your reward.

Cast your burden on Him,
and leave it there,
and then begin to realize,
that it's now His care.

He calmed the storm before,
and He'll do it again,
because you belong to Him,
and now are kin.

JUNE 4

THE NARROW PATH

It's easy to see,
for the path is wide.
Many are on it,
walking side by side.

The path extends,
throughout each country.
Within view of all,
it's easy to see.

Over mountains it goes,
and through valleys deep,
it's easy to find,
if that's what you seek.

It's disguised as nice,
and tries to attract,
would-be travelers,
to follow its track.

Don't worry about space.
There's always room,
but I warn you now,
it leads to Hell's gloom.

Then there's another path,
much narrower in form,
that many won't walk,
and will only take scorn.

It's there for all,
but the majority refuse,
and will not walk it,
in their own personal shoes.

Many insincere hearts,
will at it laugh,
but an earnest heart,
will find this path.

This path leads,
to a wonderful place,
but to walk this path,
one must receive God's grace.

Come to Jesus,
and acceptance do make,
and get on the path,
that leads to Heaven's gate.

JUNE 5

DREAMS COME TRUE

I had a dream.
It was just last night.
I was on a white horse,
and moving in flight.

On the lead horse sat,
the King of Kings.
I could spot Him,
from the way I leaned.

He led the charge,
back to earth,
leading many riders,
across space of great girth.

As we approached earth,
I quickly knew,
we were heading for Israel,
as it came into view.

Prior to the rapture,
I had read,
about the Battle of Armageddon,
and what the prophet said.

The armies of the world,
were before us all,
as we continued to listen,
for the Lord's call.

The battle was fought,
upon the Lord's shout.
Victory was complete,
leaving no doubt.

The millennium was here,
just as the Bible said.
I had remembered it,
from what I had read.

Morning did come,
and then I awoke.
I then listened to my heart,
and to what it spoke.

Dreams come true,
is what I heard,
for you know this story,
is in the Word.

JUNE 6

DOUBLE CROSSED

The coven did meet,
on this October night,
preparing a child sacrifice,
that will be killed with a knife.

To honor their god,
Satan by name,
and perform acts of abomination,
that will be done without shame.

Demons do gather,
with great delight,
to watch closely,
at this isolated site.

Perversion takes place,
ghastly acts of vice.
Anyone can see,
it's not very nice.

The Satanists delight,
and so they believe,
in their source,
from whom they've received.

Deceived they are,
although they don't know,
that damnation awaits,
when to Hell they will go.

When they arrive,
there will be great surprise,
but it'll be too late,
for they believed Satan's lies.

They will cry out,
"Satan, I served you well."
But, Satan, just used them,
now, "Welcome to Hell."

Torment will take place,
and they'll have much mental pain,
when they realize their reward,
and what they gained.

Thoughts will go back,
to the message of salvation,
and how they refused it,
to accept eternal damnation.

JUNE 7

DON'T TAKE THE MARK

The Beast will rise,
during the period of tribulation,
and he'll use a mark,
to bring people under domination.

The Beast will use numbers,
that will have "666",
to serialize on the body,
and to it affix.

To function in society,
this mark will be required,
by order of decree,
even if not desired.

The Bible is clear,
on the "Mark of the Beast".
Don't take the mark,
whether great or least.

I don't say this quietly,
but I speak with a shout.
Look in the Bible,
if you have any doubt.

To take the mark,
will seal one's fate,
for if it's ever taken,
it'll be too late.

Now listen real carefully,
I want you to hear,
"It'll be too late for salvation."
Let's be totally clear.

Refuse the mark,
I say again,
and accept the Lord Jesus,
and repent from sin.

A martyr's death,
perhaps awaits,
but because of God's grace,
it isn't too late.

Receive these words,
that I do proclaim,
and the Book of Life,
will record your name.

JUNE 8

BULLDOG FAITH

Get close to a dog,
if he has a new bone,
and he'll likely growl,
or turn and be gone.

The growl confirms,
and serves as a good sign,
that the bone belongs to him,
at least in his mind.

Try to take it,
if you dare,
but be forewarned,
to do it with care.

It's a prize,
that the dog wants to keep.
You know it's true,
if his bone you do seek.

No loose bite here,
as you observe this site.
He shows determination,
as he holds on tight.

We must use faith,
in a similar vein,
as we stand on God's Word,
and to it lay claim.

We must not change words,
to our song,
but must stand firm,
and stay real strong.

Determined we are,
to receive our prize,
as we expect to see it,
before our eyes.

JUNE 9

FOUNDATION

Before a house is built,
the foundation is laid,
to provide support,
before additions are made.

A strong base is important,
a point I must make,
for a foundation built wrong,
could prove a great mistake.

The house may crumble,
when force does come,
for the foundation was weak,
and the walls had to succumb.

To lay a new foundation,
could come at great cost.
It's often not considered,
until there comes great lost.

A word I do have,
for one who has an ear.
Consider these words spiritually,
of what you're about to hear.

Doctrine lays a foundation,
and must be built with truth,
for if it's built wrong,
it may not support your roof.

Your life's blueprint is important.
Does it follow God's plan,
or does it go contrary,
and follow a plan of man?

Doctrine is important,
make no mistake.
So get your foundation right,
before it becomes too late.

JUNE 10

POT OF GOLD

Life's pot of gold,
many people do seek,
as they chase after rainbows,
and their colors so neat.

Trace the arch,
to the colors' end.
It should be there,
after the final bend.

People try that,
and people try this,
but no pot of gold,
again they miss.

Many try to do,
things which they're not called,
and this is the reason,
that many do fall.

Dreams are dreams,
but can be true,
when you know your talent,
and what you should do.

In all human beings,
talents have been placed,
but they need to be developed,
under God's grace.

Find your talent,
and develop it well.
It's within you,
to you I will tell.

Closely examine yourself,
and look within.
Your talent is there,
on this you can depend.

Satisfaction is gained,
when your talent is known,
for it provides a key note,
to your life's song.

Searching for a pot of gold,
one worth your weight,
then find and develop your talent.
It's never too late.

JUNE 11

TAKE A HOT BATH

Fill the bathtub,
and make it hot.
Don't want it cold,
ensure it's not.

Run the water,
and make it hot.
Avoid lukewarm,
ensure it's not.

A nice hot bath,
is my request.
It's my preference,
I will attest.

An idea comes,
when I think of this,
one that I will share,
so you won't miss.

When you get in the tub,
and the water's tepid,
you'll probably run more hot,
to eliminate insipid.

As you run more hot,
think of this.
Now here it is,
that I will list.

Look in the Bible,
and turn to Revelations.
Look into Chapter Three,
for this illumination.

The Lord does not want,
Christians to be lukewarm,
but He wants them on fire,
to avoid His scorn.

So when you take your next bath,
consider His words,
and meditate on them,
all that you've heard.

Run the water,
and make it hot.
Avoid lukewarm,
ensure it's not.

JUNE 12

DANGER SIGNS

Slippery when wet,
or watch for dangerous curve,
pay attention to road signs,
to prevent dangerous swerves.

Caution ahead,
men at work.
Better slow your vehicle,
and remain alert.

Yield to traffic,
there's a lane coming in.
Better proceed with caution,
in order to blend.

Traffic signs serve as warnings,
as you well know,
to prevent accidents,
where vehicles go.

Towards your way,
these words are sent,
to consider them spiritually,
as they do give hint.

The desire to worship,
and gather in His Name,
provides one sign,
when it starts to wane.

The busy schedule,
throughout the day,
provides another sign,
when there's no time to pray.

Studying the Word,
a thing of the past.
Better rekindle interest,
and not let it last.

The message is here,
and should be clear.
Return to the things,
you once held dear.

Remember how it was,
when you were first saved.
Return to those things,
throughout each day.

JUNE 13

GREATER IS HE

Today many people focus,
on the devil and his crowd,
magnifying his efforts,
expressing fear out loud.

Watch out for the devil,
he's a mean old sort.
They'll hear his voice,
and believe his negative reports.

The devil has them on the run,
just listen to their cries.
It's so unfortunate,
that they believe his lies.

The Bible clearly states,
that truth will set you free.
So if you believe the devil,
then please listen to me.

Greater is God.
This is no contest.
He's superior in every way,
while the devil is infinitely less.

God is greater,
much greater than the devil,
and He only wants good for you,
and not the devil's evil.

Take God at His Word,
and let it light your lamp,
and then begin to realize,
that He's in your camp.

Magnify God,
and expect to receive.
Don't listen to the devil,
and become deceived.

God is greater,
and He loves you so much.
So open up your heart,
and receive His touch.

God's Word delivers,
as you trust in Him.
Every promise is true,
each and every one of them.

JUNE 14

TAXI

The taxi arrives,
as you signal by sound,
to pick you up,
and take you cross town.

The driver asks,
as you tell him your destination.
He then turns and drives,
to get you to that location.

Away he goes,
down numerous streets,
as you sit and watch,
from the back seat.

Somehow you arrive,
through twists and turns.
It reminds me of the Word,
and something I learned.

The taxi is a vehicle,
to get you to a place.
It's the same with your words,
I'll explain without haste.

In the spiritual realm,
your words carry weight.
They affect your life,
of which I'll accentuate.

Your tongue is a rudder,
it steers your ship.
So choose your words carefully,
before they leave your lips.

Your words have an impact,
don't fool yourself.
They'll affect your destination,
when your mouth they've left.

Your words are important,
again I stress.
They'll bring victory or defeat,
during life's tests.

The taxi is here,
so please get in.
Now give your destination,
and where your trip will end.

JUNE 15

NOAH'S ARK

Evidence has shown,
the remnants of an ark.
Found on top of Mt. Ararat,
this isn't a lark.

Eyewitnesses have seen,
with their own physical eyes,
an ark set in glacier,
one of good size.

Wood taken from the ark,
brought back by man,
is clearly foreign,
to the ground of this land.

It traces back in time,
to years before,
to around Noah's time.
Need I say more.

I submit to you,
that this story is true,
and it's backed by the Bible,
if you want a clue.

The Bible does state,
to be a fact,
that the ark did settle,
on top of Mt. Ararat.

I think it interesting,
and choose to say,
that God left it in view,
for these latter days.

Many scientists are befuddled,
and find it hard to explain,
why this ark is there,
and from where it came.

Turn to the Bible,
and your answer will be,
right before your eyes.
So open them and see.

Science tries to explain life,
and I'll try not to be uncouth,
but don't let science rob you,
of the gospel truth.

Sorry, Mr. Darwin,
I have a better source,
and I'm quite sure,
He didn't take your course.

The Bible is true,
contrary to evolution.
So accept Jesus as Lord,
for life's eternal solution.

JUNE 16

ROB THE WORD

Approaches are consistently made,
often from different angles,
to rob the Word,
by the devil's angels.

Traps are planned,
and snares are cast,
to rob good seed,
along one's path.

Get that seed,
out of the man's heart.
Don't let it grow,
but ensure it departs.

The objective is clear,
for the devil knows well,
that the Word is a weapon,
against the works of Hell.

Keep the man in darkness,
to his demons he tells.
Try strife and division,
where the man does dwell.

Don't let that seed grow.
Try sickness as a device,
to rob that seed,
and pull the heist.

Rob that seed,
for the demons do know,
that it'll affect their kingdom,
if it's allowed to grow.

The man becomes a threat,
when good seed grows in his heart.
That's why demons work hard,
to get it to depart.

Learn this point,
and let it sink in,
that Satan goes after the Word,
as trials he will send.

So remain steadfast,
and water it well,
and you'll gain the victory,
over the hosts of Hell.

JUNE 17

A LONELY WALK

The walk of faith,
is often a lonely walk,
where you stand alone,
and maintain your talk.

Others may not support,
or see it your way,
but steadfast you must be,
in all you say.

God's promises are true,
in your heart they were sown.
You've continued to water them,
and now they've grown.

Set your face as flint,
for you won't be denied.
You've confidence in God's Word,
for you know He didn't lie.

You know that you know,
it will come to pass.
Although circumstances say different,
they'll be changed and won't last.

Encourage your heart,
and let it be known,
that you'll continue to stand,
no matter how long.

Continue to proclaim,
that victory is ahead,
opposing worldly thoughts,
sent from your head.

You're believing God's words,
and your actions correspond.
You won't be swindled by Satan,
or believe his cons.

So walk your walk,
and on this I purport,
that God won't let you down,
even when others don't support.

There's one walking with you,
not perceived by them,
for you know victory's ahead,
as you rest in Him.

JUNE 18

DON'T TAKE THE BAIT

The fisherman takes his hook,
and on it places bait.
He then casts his line,
and begins to wait.

Watching his line,
he waits for a bass,
to take the lure,
of his line cast.

Observe he will,
trying to snare,
a deceived fish,
if he'll dare.

The bait looks good,
and so he thought,
as the fish took it,
and now is caught.

The devil also observes,
as he throws out bait,
watching for takers,
as he does wait.

He whispers softly,
words of deceit,
and then begins to watch,
from a front row seat.

Will he take it,
and to temptation latch?
For if he does,
into sin he'll be snatched.

It's very interesting,
for the man thinks it's him,
thinking his own thoughts,
each and every one of them.

If he only knew,
that this was not so,
perhaps it would affect the outcome,
and the way he would go.

Thoughts are personalized,
and by demons tactfully placed,
to upset one's walk,
and affect one's race.

JUNE 19

NO PREJUDICE HERE

Prejudice is real.
Check out all nations.
You can usually find some form,
to prevent full integration.

Sometimes it's skin color,
or religious division,
that brings out prejudice,
and acts of derision.

No entrance here.
You belong to the wrong gang.
Things of this nature,
bring great shame.

Wars are fought,
and lives are lost,
from the hands of prejudice,
that brings great cost.

It's different with God.
He's a God of great love.
That's why he sent,
His Son from above.

No matter your skin color,
or your particular race,
all are invited,
to receive God's grace.

You may be big,
or you may be small.
God loves each of you,
both one and all.

There's no prejudice in God.
He says to men of all nations,
receive Jesus as Lord,
and His gift of salvation.

JUNE 20

GIVE IT UP

Give it up,
don't cling to it.
The best thing to do,
is to just let go of it.

Give it up,
it's really hurting you.
Give it up,
it's what you should do.

Give it up,
it's robbing your peace.
Don't retain it,
but release.

Give it up,
and from its grip go.
It's hurting you more,
than you really know.

Give it up,
for if you neglect,
it'll affect your life,
with strangling effects.

Give it up,
don't hold unforgiveness.
It'll work against you,
with its taste of bitterness.

Give it up,
and slip away,
from its binding tugs,
that'll bring dismay.

Follow the Bible,
and walk in its light,
for to harbor unforgiveness,
it just isn't right.

JUNE 21

ENTER AND EXIT

Two things are common,
throughout your years.
You enter and exit,
so now please hear.

Into a house you go,
and then come out.
You enter and exit,
there's sure no doubt.

Into a car you go,
and then come out.
You enter and exit,
there's sure no doubt.

Into a building you go,
and then come out.
You enter and exit,
there's sure no doubt.

Into a store you go,
and then come out.
You enter and exit,
there's sure no doubt.

The picture is clear,
by now you see,
you enter and exit,
so listen to me.

You enter this life,
as a newborn child,
and someday you'll exit,
no matter what style.

All will exit,
it's part of life.
No need to argue,
and get in strife.

You're going to leave.
Accept it as fact.
Evidence supports this,
there is no lack.

So when you leave,
I hope you know,
where you stand with God,
and where you'll go.

JUNE 22

DECLARE THE POWER OF GOD

God can be trusted,
so I will arise.
I'll continue to trust him,
and of myself revive.

Disappointments may come,
and delays are real,
but I'll continue to trust Him,
for I have a covenant seal.

Let it be said,
He won't let me down,
for His eyes are upon me,
as He listens to my heart's sounds.

My answer is coming,
for my heart has cried out.
The manifestation will come,
of this I will not doubt.

I declare the power of God,
"Disappointment be gone."
I'll continue to stand,
no matter how long.

I declare the power of God,
"Adversity be removed."
I'll continue to stand,
and will go through.

I declare the power of God,
"I'll be delivered."
I'll continue to stand,
and of oppression will sever.

I declare the power of God,
"Victory is mine."
I'll continue to stand,
and of its fruits will dine.

I've addressed the circumstances,
and have placed a demand,
using the promises of God,
to make my stand.

I refuse to quit,
for I know my Lord,
and will continue to stand,
and trust in His Word.

JUNE 23

FREEDOM

Freedom is to be valued,
the right to choose,
the right to gain,
and the right to lose.

A prisoner behind bars,
will often lament,
desiring his freedom,
with gripping sentiment.

So many people,
under a dictatorship,
long for freedom's drink,
even if for a sip.

A quality exists,
that's hard to explain,
but if it's lost,
it causes inner pain.

It's part of man's being,
to want to be free,
woven into his nature,
where one doesn't see.

The Master Craftsman did ordain,
as He drew up His plan,
that freedom's desire,
would be incorporated into man.

The right to choose,
came with the desire of freedom,
and based upon this right,
man would come into God's kingdom.

Salvation would come,
through freedom of choice.
It would not be demanded,
or even forced.

JUNE 24

THE MIGHTY OAK

If given a choice,
to be a tree,
what would you choose,
what would it be?

Look around you,
many types exist.
Review your choices,
go down your list.

The willow sways,
in a stiff wind.
Look at its branches,
and you'll see them bend.

It's not the only one,
that bends this way.
As you look at others,
you'll see them sway.

Now consider the oak,
and how its roots go deep,
and its mighty trunk,
and the stability it keeps.

Let the rain come,
and let the wind blow,
and watch the mighty oak,
and the strength it shows.

A lesson is here,
for us to perceive,
as we look at the oak,
let us receive.

In the storm,
when the weather goes wrong,
as a picture of strength,
it stands up strong.

JUNE 25

SCALES WILL BE BALANCED

Sometimes it may seem,
from the eyes of the Christian,
that many ungodly greatly prosper,
but now please listen.

What you're doing for Christ,
hasn't gone unnoticed.
God maintains accurate books,
and keeps good lists.

Continue to be diligent,
in the great commission,
and maintain your course,
as a good Christian.

Work for God,
and on your course endure,
for rewards will come.
It's for sure.

Trust and do His Word,
and blessings will come.
He won't let you down.
Consider it done.

God balances the books,
in this life and next.
So please take heed,
as you read this text.

Don't envy the ungodly,
but do it God's way,
for the scales will be balanced.
Listen to what I say.

So encourage yourself,
and lift up your chin.
Blessings will be yours,
as you trust in Him.

JUNE 26

PARACHUTIST

The parachutist gets on the airplane,
before it takes flight,
as he takes his parachute,
that can be used during day or night.

The airplane takes off,
as the engines roar,
into the sky it goes,
and begins to soar.

The drop zone is near,
as the parachutist looks out.
He has confidence in his parachute,
and does not doubt.

As the parachutist jumps,
and the canopy deploys,
he floats through the sky,
and the ride he enjoys.

Consider man's life,
after he is born.
It's like a parachutist,
that went airborne.

The airplane flies at different levels,
throughout its flight,
as it can change directions,
during day or night.

Yet, the parachutist will depart,
during that flight.
Not dependent on time,
it could be day or night.

As in life,
one will die,
like the parachutist that leaves the airplane,
and departs into the sky.

His parachute protects him,
and with safety covers,
as he falls to the earth,
and under canopy hovers.

When you make the jump,
and from this earth depart,
make sure you have your parachute,
by accepting Jesus into your heart.

JUNE 27

WALLS

Walls come in different sizes.
Some are low,
and some are high,
as far as walls go.

Walls are made of different materials.
Some are brick,
and some are wood,
where placed to sit.

They all serve a purpose.
Some are for protective defense,
while others may be seen around a garden,
as a masonry fence.

Walls of the heart,
equally serve a role,
made of different materials,
but cast in similar molds.

Walls of unforgiveness,
grip the inner soul.
Refusing to release things,
they maintain a strong hold.

Walls of bitterness,
bite like a chilling wind.
As it says in the Bible,
this amounts to sin.

Walls of envy,
need to be broken down.
Push them all over,
until they fall to the ground.

Walls of inadequacy,
need to be pushed aside,
for people are the righteousness of God,
if in Christ they abide.

Walls of hurt feelings,
are not good to build.
They'll rob the heart,
and of joy will steal.

Don't allow these walls to stand,
but continue to chisel with love.
It's the prescription for inner healing,
sent to you from above.

JUNE 28

A PUDDLE IS FORMING

Rain just started,
a few minutes ago.
The street is getting wet,
as wetness is beginning to show.

It has been an hour now,
and a puddle is beginning to form,
as the rain has increased,
from the spring storm.

As I observe the puddle,
it makes me think,
of the devil's actions,
and how they link.

Plans are made,
and thoughts are sent,
trying to plant seeds,
with ill intent.

If the seed is taken,
the devil will return,
to carefully water it,
as it wasn't spurned.

With each visit,
the seed will grow,
where it'll become evident,
as actions will show.

As you observe the person,
and how his problem grew,
remember the puddle,
when you do.

It has been three hours now,
and the puddle has grown.
So it can be with a seed,
after it's sown.

JUNE 29

FISHING FOR MEN

A fisherman fishes,
with a goal in mind,
to catch a fish,
in reasonable time.

He baits his hook,
with something appealable,
so that it attracts,
and makes the fish agreeable.

He casts his line,
and then he waits,
for the fish to come,
and take the bait.

Learning from this lesson,
would be wise,
for it applies to men,
no matter what size.

Say for example,
you run into a man,
that likes football,
you know where he stands.

Perhaps it's hunting,
that rings his bell.
You now have a lead in,
for the gospel to tell.

Computers he likes,
well, now you know,
how to hook up with him,
and the way to go.

People like to talk,
about things they enjoy.
It's part of human nature,
whether man or boy.

Rapport is established,
in this kind of approach.
Now look to the Holy Spirit,
who'll serve as your coach.

As He leads you,
share the message of salvation.
It's a wonderful message,
needed in all nations.

JUNE 30

FLIGHT COMING IN

Get to the airport,
and check the gate,
and also the arrival time,
in case it's late.

Sometimes delays occur,
caused by fog or snow,
causing one to wonder,
if the flight will show.

The flight typically comes in,
even if a delay has occurred,
making one think,
of God's Holy Word.

Prayer is made,
and sent are petitions,
seeking God's help,
for divine intervention.

People get excited,
and will quickly pray,
wanting to see the manifestation,
without slightest delay.

Spiritual warfare occurs,
as we remember in the Book of Daniel,
when the answer was sent,
and was to be delivered by God's angel.

Demonic opposition arose,
to withstand the angel,
but the angel broke through,
to get to Daniel.

As one prays,
one must remember,
that spiritual warfare occurs,
and not to simmer.

God is faithful,
He knows your address.
So don't get uptight,
and full of stress.

Your answer has been sent,
it's coming your way.
Just continue to trust Him,
and don't dismay.

JULY 1

RELEASE YOUR FRUITS

Within each Christian,
fruits are placed,
placed by God,
to share with the human race.

Love is shown,
that often accompanies kindness,
while people take note,
of a certain goodness.

Joy is seen,
as people perceive gentleness,
in the lives of Christians,
as they maintain their faithfulness.

Peace is observed,
as self-control is displayed,
in everyday living,
and circumstances of dismay.

Patience is evident,
as Christians stand,
on the promises of God,
and not the humanism of man.

The fruits are there,
and should be shared,
in a violent world,
that needs to know God cares.

Each fruit has a place,
and can minister to others.
So hide them not in a basket,
and attempt to smother.

Let your fruits come forth,
and boldly proclaim,
the grace of God,
with much acclaim.

Lives will be affected,
and will never be the same,
after they've been touched by God,
and have had their hearts changed.

Release your fruits,
again I say.
So start right now,
and begin today!

JULY 2

A NEW COAT

Snow is falling.
It's beginning to cover the ground.
Silence fills the air,
as there appears to be little sound.

One perceives a change,
as one views this scene.
So now sharpen your wits,
and make them keen.

Grass is being covered,
and trees as well,
with a new coat of white,
as the scene does tell.

It's such a different site,
from that of before,
a dramatic change,
if one kept score.

When Jesus forgives,
He takes the spots away,
from a sin-filled heart,
that went astray.

Washed away are these sins,
and never to be remembered,
for they're been placed under the blood,
like ground covered with snow in December.

Sin is washed away,
as the spirit becomes as white as snow.
It's such a dramatic change,
that all men should know.

Get a new coat,
it can be obtained from Christ,
the new coat of salvation,
that will fit so nice.

JULY 3

TOMATO PLANT

There was a tomato plant,
that lived in the shade.
He was starting to grow roots,
until a change was made.

A member of the family,
came by his way,
and decided to uproot him,
that very day.

He was placed in the sun,
into new ground,
with new surroundings,
and even new sounds.

Then another family member came by,
and stopped and looked,
and decided to uproot him,
to a garden nook.

It was hard to grow roots,
moving to and fro.
Just when he started,
it was time to go.

No fruit was grown,
as a result of the moves,
but a moral exists,
that we don't want to lose.

Many people go,
from church to church,
uprooting themselves,
and moving much.

Roots aren't grown,
deep into the earth,
making it hard,
for fruit to be birthed.

God has a place,
make no mistake,
for people to worship,
and a church home to make.

Growth will take place,
as roots are set down,
bringing forth fruit,
that will abound.

JULY 4

REMEMBER THE CLOWN

Go to the rodeo,
and watch the clown,
or to the circus,
if it's in town.

He makes people laugh,
as he moves around,
doing funny things,
because he's a clown.

Look at the children,
and watch their faces,
as the clown acts funny,
and goes through his paces.

When the event is over,
and the children depart,
they leave happily,
with merry hearts.

They feel so good,
because they went.
You can be assured,
it was time well spent.

Laughter is good,
perhaps you've been told,
of the medicinal affect,
it has on one's soul.

So when something upsets,
and it comes with frown,
remember this little story,
about the clown.

Put a smile on your face,
and don't be downcast.
Lighten up and laugh,
and the frown will pass.

JULY 5

STRONG GRIP

I will never leave you.
I will never forsake you,
throughout all trials and tribulations,
no matter what comes against you.

This is God speaking.
So don't forget,
that's it's totally true,
when you ponder it.

God is trustworthy.
Have confidence in Him,
during all adverse situations,
each and every one of them.

Take a hammer,
and have a strong man grip it.
It may be tight,
but over you God has a greater grip.

Forget not the past,
when He delivered you.
He'll do it again,
and bring you through.

Forget not the past,
when He blessed you.
He'll do it again,
and bring you through.

Cast not away your confidence,
for He is faithful.
Be assured He's there,
so remain grateful.

Sense His grip,
it's stronger than strong,
He won't let go,
for to Him you belong.

JULY 6

DISTORTION OF FOCUS

Use a magnifying glass,
and the size appears to increase.
Move the magnifying glass further away,
and the size appears to decrease.

The moon appears to come closer,
when using a telescope,
as a microbe appears larger,
under a microscope.

The size of these items,
does not change.
It's a matter of focus,
using technical gains.

Appearance can be deceiving,
depending on where you look,
as information will vary,
in different books.

One hears a story,
and draws certain conclusions,
and then magnifies it greatly,
out of proportion.

Another hears the story,
and does the same.
Pretty soon this spreads,
and ruins a good name.

Distortion is made,
as gossip is passed,
twisting the truth,
while slander is cast.

Is this good?
I think not so.
So ignore the gossip,
and do not sow.

Instead, focus on the good,
and these things discuss.
Yes, spread good words,
and the gossip hush.

Know this is right,
and is the better way,
to focus your attention,
on good words to say.

JULY 7

GOD'S NUMBER ONE BUSINESS

God's number one business,
in North America,
is exactly the same,
for South America.

God's number one business,
in the Far East,
is exactly the same,
for the Near East.

It's exactly the same,
all across Russia,
as it is in Europe,
or throughout Africa.

God's number one business,
is that of restoration.
The process begins,
with that of salvation.

If you need redemption,
then come to the Lord.
He wants you restored,
as it says in His Word.

If you need deliverance,
then come to the Lord.
He wants you restored,
as it says in His Word.

If you need healing,
then come to the Lord.
He wants you restored,
as it says in His Word.

Whatever it is,
God has met the need.
Restoration begins,
through the Blood of Calvary.

JULY 8

FACADE

Props are used,
to make movie scenes.
They look so real,
on the television screen.

Towns are built,
as they erect facades,
creating illusions,
like the devil against God.

Illusions aren't real,
but they're perceived as such.
They're like circumstantial evidence,
which the devil uses much.

When the devil comes calling,
remember he's the Father of Lies,
don't be deceived,
and give him your eyes.

God's Word takes precedence,
over the devil's illusions.
So always side with the truth,
for the biblical solution.

Resist the fiery darts,
and negative reports.
Speak the Word against Satan,
and all his cohort.

Don't dwell on defeat,
while deliverance is yours.
It's written in blood,
that makes victory sure.

Don't believe the illusions,
and settle for less,
but be bold in the truth,
that brings God's best.

JULY 9

ON A TIGER'S BACK

Tigers can be ferocious,
most people will agree.
Just watch their behavior,
and then you'll see.

Playing with a tiger,
could ruin your day,
I would advise against it,
listen to what I say.

Yet people will approach,
and get on a tiger's back,
demonstrating poor judgment,
and wisdom that lacks.

A dangerous ride is in store,
as they hold on tight,
but then it's hard to get off,
try as they might.

Run with cocaine,
or perhaps a heroin drug,
and you'll quickly find,
it has a tight hug.

Get into occult,
and play its game,
and you'll quickly find,
it'll bring much shame.

Involved in adultery,
and playing with fire,
you're apt to get burnt,
along with your lustful desires.

Want to get on a tiger's back?
Now please don't scoff,
but if you get on,
it can be hard to get off.

Appealing it may seem,
but I will advise,
that the ride isn't worth it,
but you have to decide.

Whatever the sin,
it has its rewards.
Better to shun its ride,
and stay with the Lord.

JULY 10

LOAD YOUR PANTRY

On pantry shelves,
provisions are placed,
often enclosed,
to keep them safe.

As food is stored,
it makes one think,
of an important point,
with a spiritual link.

If one needs food,
to the pantry one goes,
to take from it,
as one would suppose.

Physical needs are met,
as food is there,
but they wouldn't have been,
if the cupboards were bare.

Trials will come,
and tests will show,
and during these times,
to the spirit one goes.

What's been stored,
in the pantry of one's heart?
Let us take a look,
into all its parts.

Are the shelves filled,
with that of good seed,
stocked with God's Word,
to meet the need?

Are the shelves bare,
or filled with trash?
Then one will have nothing,
no need to rehash.

Fill your heart's pantry,
and fill it well,
with the Word of God,
and on His promises dwell.

Then food will be there,
to answer the need,
to rise up strong,
from a supply of good seed.

JULY 11

POKER GAME

Check his face,
as he looks at the cards.
Now watch his hands,
as he prepares to discard.

Check for signs,
to reveal his hand.
Watch him closely,
as much as you can.

As you observe,
you can't read his mind,
but you can watch for signals,
as you look for signs.

Demons watch you,
in a similar vein,
looking for ways,
to make some gain.

They can't read minds,
but they'll watch you well,
devising schemes,
inspired from Hell.

They'll send fiery darts,
thoughts of defeat.
Now watch the face,
will he keep?

Will he side with the Word,
and not give way,
or will he begin to worry,
and show great dismay?

The man's mind,
it may quake a bit,
but if he rests in the Word,
he won't show it.

Baffled they'll be,
when he stands real strong,
and frightened they'll be,
when he sends them along.

The cards are dealt,
now watch the face.
Remember these words,
as you run your race.

JULY 12

DON'T BACK DOWN

The Israelites gathered,
in battle array,
across from the Philistines,
on that historical day.

Goliath came forth,
and taunted with call,
as the Israelites cowered,
from the giant they saw.

A shepherd boy heard,
the taunts of this giant,
but refused to accept them,
and became defiant.

Is there not a cause,
to face this giant?
He trusted in God,
for knew He was reliant.

To Saul he went,
to let him hear,
that he would go forth,
and would volunteer.

David charged out,
on that fateful day,
as he did battle,
and the giant did slay.

David gained victory,
as he trusted God.
It was with God's help,
that he beat all odds.

Giants in the natural,
are certainly real,
but remember God,
and your covenant seal.

Put that stone,
into your sling.
Then wind it up,
and let it fling.

Stand on the Word,
and speak it out.
Then begin to voice,
your victory shout.

JULY 13

AROUND THE CLOCK

Man needs sleep,
it's commonly known,
whether it be young,
or fully grown.

Mankind knows,
the body needs rest,
some more so,
and some a little less.

God is different,
to say the least,
ever awake,
it doesn't cease.

Around the clock,
He's awake,
able to watch over you,
for your sake.

Protection is available,
around the clock,
for those that claim it,
and on God's door knock.

Come to Him,
and claim His protection.
Know for sure,
you won't face rejection.

Put Him in remembrance,
and let Him know,
that you want His protection,
wherever you go.

Rock solid protection,
now is yours.
Around the clock,
you can feel secure.

Peril may hit,
on your street.
While others may fall,
you stay on your feet.

You know Psalm 91,
and have proclaimed,
its words of protection,
in His precious Name.

JULY 14

ALL THE MONEY

Gather all the money,
from all the lands.
Take it all,
from all the men.

Put it together,
all in one place,
for it will demonstrate,
the glory of God's grace.

Keep it coming,
billions upon billions.
Let it continue to mount,
trillions upon trillions.

Now that we have it,
let's invite the Lord,
to come and visit,
this wealth of hoard.

A proposal we have,
for the King of Kings,
as He now arrives,
at this scene.

Let's propose to the Lord,
to buy one soul,
with all this money,
and all this gold.

He's ready to respond,
and His answer is no.
It's in line with the Bible,
as we should well know.

All the money in the world,
could not buy one soul.
It's more precious to Him,
than all the earth's gold.

God's love is deep,
for each and every man,
no matter what country,
no matter what land.

The priorities of God,
are different from man's.
In relation to His,
where do ours stand?

JULY 15

SPARK PLUG

Turn the key,
ignition kicks in,
helped by the sparks,
down in the engine.

Just a little help,
from the sparks,
got the car going,
and off to its start.

Sometimes people,
just need a spark,
to get them up,
when things appear dark.

Check some faces,
in your town.
You'll see distress,
and many frowns.

A kind word here,
and a kind word there,
may provide a spark,
to lift their care.

So let your voice,
make proclamation,
of encouraging words,
and exhortation.

Share God's love.
It's as precious pearls,
for those in need,
in a very sad world.

If the need exists,
then share Christ.
It's the perfect spark,
that brings new life.

JULY 16

I HEAR A KNOCK

There's someone,
knocking at your door,
waiting for you to open,
at your entrance floor.

He's been standing,
with deep concern,
hoping you'll answer,
and will not spurn.

Two weeks ago,
He came by,
but you sent Him away,
with no reply.

He loves you much,
if you only knew,
the love of this one,
that keeps visiting you.

I hear you say,
with words of your mouth,
that no one came,
to your house.

Well let me say,
my words are true.
It's at your heart's door,
where He visited you.

Your heart has a door,
I will proclaim.
It's there He visited you,
Jesus by name.

You must open it,
for Him to come in,
to provide salvation,
and to cleanse you from sin.

To keep it closed,
would not be wise.
Oh, it hurts Him so,
and brings tears to His eyes.

For to keep it closed,
will bring damnation,
as you spurn His love,
and eternal salvation.

JULY 17

SQUARE PEG

Take a square peg,
and place into a round hole.
You'll notice it doesn't fit,
if I may be so bold.

It's obvious to see,
the peg does not fit,
even if pushed,
and with pressure hit.

Push as you will,
push as you may,
you'll see it won't work,
just as I say.

Take a look at the church,
and remember this drill,
as we turn over some dirt,
and begin to till.

People come to church,
and get gloriously saved,
but then they must learn,
how to behave.

Renewal of mind,
is certainly required,
if one is to mature,
as one desires.

The world's system,
has had its affect,
after years without the Lord,
and of spiritual neglect.

Square pegs,
have to be shaped,
to slide into round holes,
and of proper fit make.

The spirit was reborn,
but the mind was not.
It still has baggage,
it has not forgot.

Get into the Word,
and think as God thinks.
Your walk will improve,
for there is a link.

JULY 18

DEVIL'S FAIRY TALE

This story started out,
from the devil of old.
He came up with this story,
to try and take men's souls.

The devil used false teachers,
to help get it out,
to say there's "no Hell",
and of true doctrine doubt.

This story spread quickly,
as a belief among man.
It made him feel good,
to have no consequences from sin.

Many children believe fairy tales,
but they're only make believe.
Many adults believe this fairy tale,
and have been totally deceived.

The Bible is clear,
and has much to say,
about when life is gone,
and a coming Judgment Day.

The Bible is clear,
there is a Hell.
This is truth,
and no fairy tale.

Payment for sin,
it is required,
but it need not be this way,
if you desire.

God wants reconciliation,
and has provided a way of escape.
Accept Jesus as Lord,
and come through Heaven's gates.

JULY 19

CONTENDER OR PRETENDER

America is proclaimed,
as a Christian nation,
where many acknowledge God,
in some kind of relation.

Then I scan the map,
and look around,
and notice something interesting,
in most towns.

By taking a look,
at patterns of behavior,
I quickly realize,
where Jesus is Savior.

From my scan,
I've noted contenders,
and equally so,
I've spotted pretenders.

There are those,
that share God's name,
and there are those,
that use it in vain.

There are those,
that gather in praise,
and there are those,
that avoid it always.

There are those,
that pursue their faith,
and there are those,
that seek to escape.

After observing some people,
I've quickly deduced,
that the meaning of Christian,
is defined as loose.

To call oneself a Christian,
does not make it so.
There's so much more,
that one must know.

One must receive Christ,
this isn't a game.
To casually pretend,
would be to die in shame.

JULY 20

GOLDEN THREADS

A garment is woven,
with different threads,
either from hand,
or machine fed.

Each has a part,
with a role to play,
blended into fabric,
much like chambray.

Created were you,
in your mother's womb,
much like fabric,
on a clothing loom.

Talents were woven,
into your frame,
different from others,
and sometimes same.

Abilities were woven,
thread by thread,
into your being,
to include head.

As complete fabric,
is seen on the shelf,
it's like an analogy,
when you look at self.

You see a total picture,
but there's so much more.
This can be easily seen,
when you look into core.

Things were woven,
specifically into you,
that makes you unique,
in what you do.

Use your talents,
that were woven into you,
as you follow God's plan
in all you do.

So find your niche,
in God's plan.
There's a specific place,
for every man.

JULY 21

LORD OF COMPASSION

Feeling something deeply,
often equates to passion,
such as the Lord felt,
when He walked with compassion.

As He walked,
He performed many good deeds,
moved with compassion,
to meet many people's needs.

Let the blind man see.
Let the lame man walk.
Let the deaf man hear,
and let the dumb man talk.

As the sick would gather,
by road or in field,
the Lord would minister,
and they would be healed.

Compassion He felt,
as He reached out,
to meet their needs,
and sickness cast out.

As you read the Bible,
you say that was yesterday.
Well, Jesus hasn't changed,
He's the same today.

Know for sure,
His love endures.
His compassion is great,
you can be assured.

Come with faith,
to Him today,
and He'll meet that need,
in a compassionate way.

JULY 22

MOST VALUABLE ASSET

Look at your car.
What a nice design.
It has a bright color,
and sure looks fine.

You have a nice house,
I do declare.
It has a fine design,
with a ranch flair.

Look at your furniture.
It looks so grand.
I guess you might say,
it's from a country plan.

I notice the trailer,
and your sleek boat.
It's certainly attractive,
as I clearly take note.

Most valuable assets,
are certainly yours,
but there's another one,
that will forever endure.

It has more value,
than the temporal ones.
So don't forget about it,
and never shun.

Time is spent,
to wash your car,
to keep your house,
and maintain other cares.

Now consider this more valuable asset,
in moments of leisure,
and you'll quickly realize,
it's a chest of treasure.

Your most valuable asset,
it's your spirit.
It lives forever,
so feed and nourish it.

Guard and protect it,
for it provides the key,
to your future years,
both now and in eternity.

JULY 23

THE JOURNEY

Christian, go over the mountain,
and through the valley.
Keep up your pace,
and do not dally.

Go through the forest,
and cross the stream.
Stay always alert,
to all earth's scenes.

You may get tired,
but keep on the go,
for when you arrive,
great joy will show.

After the long journey,
and trip is complete,
you'll be able to pause,
and rest your feet.

At the end of life's journey,
there'll be total celebration.
For you're in Christ,
imagine the great jubilation.

It'll be the opposite,
at journey's end,
for those that have died,
in their sins.

Journeys in life,
bring different emotions.
It'll be the same at death,
with all its commotions.

Joy for you,
for you have salvation,
but for those in sin,
there'll be great devastation.

All take life's journey,
but it's a personal decision,
if one accepts Jesus,
and the gift of salvation.

If you haven't accepted Christ,
and you want a great journey's end,
then accept Him right now,
and be redeemed from all sin.

JULY 24

TWO THIEVES

Let's go back in time,
to Christ's crucifixion,
when many turned,
and gave Him rejection.

Despised by man,
and spat upon,
was Jesus Christ,
God's only Son.

Jeers were made,
and disdain put forth,
but people didn't realize,
this was Christ's ordained course.

Two thieves there were,
that surrounded Him,
when truth took hold,
of one of them.

There they were,
each on a cross,
when one was saved,
and the other stayed lost.

The one jeered,
but the other appealed,
that Christ would remember Him,
as they died on that hill.

In a second of time,
his fate was sealed,
all because of his act,
when to Christ he appealed.

It's no different today,
when one appeals to Christ.
He's just waiting to impart,
to you eternal life.

JULY 25

REEXAMINE THE TOMB

Go to Jerusalem,
and enter Christ's tomb.
Don't worry about space,
there's plenty of room.

You'll notice it's empty,
as you make your inspection.
It's because He left,
during His resurrection.

Peter and John,
they noticed the same,
and as a result,
salvation would be claimed.

They pondered the tomb,
as they departed its site,
but soon clarity would come,
like black and white.

Upon seeing Jesus,
they began to walk,
and after Pentecost,
they began to talk.

The gospel spread,
from tongues of fire,
as the disciples were driven,
by the Lord's desires.

Separated they were,
from the things of earth,
for they had received,
the new birth.

No middle of the ground,
for this band.
They lived for Christ,
in their land.

Let us examine our lives,
and the way we walk.
Let us examine our words,
and the way we talk.

As you ponder Christ's tomb,
and its empty plot,
know you're living for Jesus,
or you're not.

JULY 26

CLOSER ORBIT

Look at the planets,
as they relate to the sun.
There's an interesting analogy,
as it relates to God's Son.

Check their orbits,
and distances involved.
It's easy to fiqure.
It's easy to solve.

A stronger pull exists,
on the planets close in.
It's caused by gravity,
and the force it sends.

So move your orbit,
closer to God's Son,
and receive greater effect,
like the planets with sun.

Don't distance yourself,
from His face,
but seek to walk closely,
under His grace.

Spend time with Him,
and stay real close.
You'll find Him to be,
a most gracious host.

Your walk will stay strong,
if you heed this advice,
but if you keep distance,
you may gain polar ice.

Check your orbit,
and get on line.
No need to delay,
it is the right time.

JULY 27

GREAT TRADE FOR YOU

Jesus has a trade,
He wants to make with you.
So let us look at this deal,
and conduct a thorough review.

He wants to first trade,
his gift of righteousness,
in exchange for your sins,
and your unworthiness.

He wants to also trade,
in exchange for your sickness,
a life of well being,
and complete healthiness.

Next on the list,
is His offer of prosperity,
in exchange for your lack,
and all your poverty.

He now offers joy,
to replace your sadness,
and if you'll trade,
then you'll receive His gladness.

What do you think?
Do you want to make this trade?
It'll be the wisest one,
you ever made.

What will it be?
Don't be a scoffer,
but take the Lord,
at His offer.

All I said,
is totally true,
but the final decision,
is up to you.

JULY 28

MINISTERIAL NOTE

Believers are apples,
apples of God's eyes.
This is said affectionately,
and not with lie.

Ministers have ministries,
because of this love.
So God monitors His ministers,
as He looks from above.

Watch over His children,
and feed His flock.
They don't belong to the minister,
this isn't a knock.

The Head of the church,
is Jesus by name.
So ministers must be careful,
if they lay claim.

They only have positions,
established by the Lord,
to care for His people,
and feed them the Word.

Ministerial positions exist.
There is one main reason.
It's because God loves people,
and wants the best for their season.

A word for ministers,
please take note.
You're there by God's grace,
so never gloat.

God is watching,
as you feed His sheep.
Remember they're His,
and in covenant He keeps.

JULY 29

CAKE COMES WITH FROSTING

Listen carefully,
as I will make,
a point about frosting,
on a cake.

Many people like it,
no matter the flavor,
and will eat the cake,
for frosting to savor.

There are nice things,
in God's Word,
but also instructions,
from the Lord.

A happy sermon,
people like to hear,
but sometimes instruction,
is not held so dear.

Bless me sermons,
are like frosting,
but there's also cake,
beneath that icing.

Corrective guidance,
comes with the package,
to help us eliminate,
the wrong baggage.

All the Word,
has a purpose,
no matter what chapter,
no matter what verse.

Receive all God's guidance.
There's value in each lesson.
We should have receptive attitudes,
during all the corrective sessions.

JULY 30

DON'T PARTAKE

The accuser of the brethren,
is Satan by name.
Don't let us partake,
and bring us shame.

There is a truth,
and towards it I'll nudge.
Let us walk in love,
and do not judge.

A multitude of sins,
is covered by love.
To walk in this way,
pleases the Father above.

The Bible says judge not,
lest you be judged.
So guard your mouth,
and do not judge.

Hardly take notice,
and do not condemn.
So they slipped,
it's better to help them.

Don't magnify their failures,
and point your finger.
Let their failures pass,
and to your mind not linger.

Sow mercy,
and be unto them kind.
In a hateful world,
this shows the right sign.

The world may judge,
and chew on the fat,
but we walk in love,
for that's where it's at.

JULY 31

GO TO THE ANT

Watch the ant,
as He works away.
Notice his diligence,
throughout the day.

A hard worker he is,
to accomplish his task.
From point to point,
you'll see him dash.

No slack here,
as he busily works.
He's getting things done,
no time to shirk.

Productive he is,
as he works real hard.
It's as if,
he doesn't get tired.

Diligence is important,
and profit will show,
an important lesson,
for us to know.

Go to the ant,
and emulate his way,
then you'll find,
you'll have a productive day.

A slothful man,
will come up short.
It's like that in life,
as the Bible reports.

Diligence at work,
and diligence in the Word,
these are things,
pleasing to the Lord.

Be a diligent man,
in all your endeavors.
Develop this habit,
and be slothful never.

AUGUST 1

COUNTENANCE

You read the pages,
when you open a book.
You can read people,
by the way they look.

The countenance reveals,
some keen insight.
As you study it,
it will shed some light.

Is there worry,
or is there sadness?
Is there peace,
or is there gladness?

Check the face,
and all expression.
You can easily tell,
if there's depression.

The face reveals,
much about one's state.
It can reveal love,
or disdain and hate.

To this I say,
be attuned,
when people walk,
into the room.

When you read a face,
of discouragement,
you can sow some seeds,
of encouragement.

Encourage in Jesus,
He's never down.
Get them to smile,
and change that frown.

It's not as bad,
as they perceive,
for things can change,
if they'll believe.

To this I say,
and should not be ignored,
Jesus wants joy,
to that soul restored.

AUGUST 2

PSEUDO PEACE

What will be will be,
so the words go.
If that was a movie,
then miss that show.

Things just happen,
and things just occur.
Don't plant your seat,
on that burr.

A prisoner of circumstances,
one need not be,
if you'll take some time,
and listen to me.

There is a fight,
the fight of faith.
A fight requires,
some effort to make.

Prayer changes things,
and also protects.
So build your faith,
and do not neglect.

You have an influence,
through your faith,
to change circumstances,
if a stand you'll take.

God's on your side,
and wants your best.
He only wants,
to see you blessed.

Don't give in,
and take a pseudo peace.
Come to the Lord,
and of your faith release.

AUGUST 3

LIKE A PAIR OF SHOES

Sizes are different,
when it comes to shoes.
You want the right size,
when you choose.

Not all shoes,
will fit your feet.
A pair not right,
you wouldn't keep.

When you go to church,
it's much the same,
when the minister speaks,
and begins to proclaim.

Many people come,
with different needs.
The Holy Spirit knows,
where to plant the right seeds.

Some things said,
may not fit your feet.
If this is true,
then don't keep.

Let it pass,
it wasn't for you.
It should be easy,
easy to do.

If the shoe fits,
then wear it.
Adjustments can be made,
from where you sit.

Different words are spoken,
from the minister's lips.
Not all may be for you,
if you want a good tip.

AUGUST 4

THE FUGITIVE

From the law,
a fugitive may run.
He may even carry,
with him a gun.

Away he flees,
out of the public's eyes.
Sometimes he may use,
even a disguise.

Free he may think,
but not really so,
for if he's detected,
he's then on the go.

Sometimes he hides,
maybe here,
and sometimes he hides,
maybe there.

He may beat the system,
and so he thinks,
but spiritually speaking,
there's an important link.

Nobody can run forever,
let this be known,
for at life's end,
one must atone.

All will stand,
before God's throne,
to provide an account,
for both good and wrong.

For those without Jesus,
the run will stop.
They won't be able to evade,
like they did life's cops.

There were tugs at their spirit,
but, no, not now,
as Christians attempted to witness,
and received fixed scowls.

The running now stops,
I say with voice.
They once had an option,
but now no choice.

AUGUST 5

TICKTOCK

Look all around you.
Israel became a nation in 1948.
Look all around you.
Man landed on the moon in 1969.

Look all around you.
It's the computer age.
Look all around you.
Technology has increased.

Look all around you.
Notice all the earthquakes.
Look all around you.
Notice all the famine.

Look all around you.
Wars have not ceased.
Look all around you.
Violence has increased.

Look all around you.
Man calls evil good.
Look all around you.
Man calls good evil.

Look all around you.
False prophets abound.
Look all around you.
People follow them.

Look, and now listen,
"Ticktock, ticktock, ticktock."
That's the sound,
of the earth's clock.

Look all around you.
Don't fool yourself.
The signs are there.
There's not much time left.

AUGUST 6

MANY TAKEN CAPTIVE

Many have been taken captive,
in the streets of the United States.
Many have perished,
but for others it's not too late.

People have been kidnapped,
right in the middle of the streets,
but answers exist,
if answers you seek.

Christians have allowed,
this nation to glide,
towards moral decadence,
on a dreadful slide.

No more school prayer,
and abortions are fine.
Just adjust to it,
and things will be fine.

Drugs are rampant,
and crime has increased.
For the health of this nation,
there must be decrease.

Mighty men of God,
need to wake up,
and stir up their spirits,
with quick alert.

It's time to take back,
and set the captives free.
This is from the heart of God,
if you'll believe me.

It's time to get serious,
and get busy in prayer.
This applies to all Christians,
whether here or there.

It's time to get serious,
and make God's work a priority.
Focus must change,
and not go along with the majority.

It's time to take back,
and restore this land.
You can be assured,
this is important to God's plan.

AUGUST 7

NO SITUATION IS HOPELESS

No situation is hopeless.
No matter the odds.
All things are possible,
through our God.

No situation is hopeless.
Don't limit the Lord.
His promises say victory,
as we stand on His Word.

No situation is hopeless.
The doctor reports cancer,
but God's counter report,
provides the right answer.

No situation is hopeless.
In God victory awaits.
Come to Him,
it's never too late.

No situation is hopeless.
Travesty may come,
but God can deliver,
if you trust in His Son.

No situation is hopeless.
God's an unlimited source.
He's able to deliver,
as you steer His course.

No situation is hopeless.
His Hand is there,
during any situation,
that comes with scare.

No situation is hopeless.
He's a big God.
No matter your situation,
He can beat all odds.

AUGUST 8

TWO ACTION WORDS

Love is an action word,
and so is faith.
Action is required for each of them,
with effort to make.

To only sit and discuss,
will make you a spectator,
but action is required,
to make you a participator.

Actions speak loud,
and will certainly confirm,
if you're using faith and love,
in the boldest of terms.

You say you have faith,
and that you believe.
Then be prepared to endure,
before you receive.

As you stand in faith,
you must maintain a good confession.
This takes effort,
and precedes your possession.

Let's take a look,
at a brother with needs.
Do you provide a casual word,
or action with deeds?

Is your schedule too busy,
to give some time?
When you walk in love,
there will be visible signs.

If you have faith and love,
then action will be seen.
As you read the Bible,
you'll see what I mean.

AUGUST 9

DEVIL'S PLAYGROUND TOYS

Let's take a visit,
to Satan's playground.
There are no carousels,
or merry-go-rounds.

Don't look for slides,
or even swings.
As you look,
you'll find different things.

Time to stop.
We're here.
Notice the bad attitude,
right over there.

Look to your left,
notice the strife.
He'll play with that,
in a person's life.

Now turn to the right.
Notice the pride.
He loves it more,
than a playground slide.

Push against this toy.
It's hard to budge.
That's because,
it's called grudge.

Jealousy and bitterness,
are next to it.
He likes to play with them,
and give people fits.

Discouragement and depression,
are just up ahead.
He'll play with them,
in peoples' heads.

You'll notice his playground toys,
have a common link.
They're played in the mind,
and they all stink.

Resist oppressive thoughts,
with bold rejection.
Don't think his way,
for your own protection.

AUGUST 10

ARE YOU READY TO WRESTLE

Wrestling is a demanding sport.
It takes endurance.
It takes stamina,
and perseverance.

Energy and effort are required,
to effectively compete.
Energy and effort are required,
to avoid defeat.

One needs to be strong,
to effectively participate.
One needs to work hard,
to achieve excellence.

The Bible tells us to fight,
the good fight of faith.
In faith there is a fight,
if you're going to participate.

It's similar to wrestling.
You have an opponent,
that resists your efforts,
towards a victorious moment.

You may get tired,
as the bout goes on,
but you must persevere,
even if it seems long.

Are you ready to wrestle?
Are you ready to come in Jesus' name,
and stand on His promises,
and victory lay claim?

You'll need to exercise your faith.
It takes endurance.
It takes stamina,
and perseverance.

Walking by faith,
is not for the weak.
You must be strong,
if victory you seek.

Are you ready to wrestle?
The promises are yours,
but you must be strong,
with faith that endures.

AUGUST 11

GROUP PHOTOGRAPH

The family assembles,
for a group photograph.
Some may even smile,
or possibly laugh.

This group is related,
as they get into position.
It's a group photograph,
as I just mentioned.

Now try and picture this,
before the camera lens.
It's the death, burial and resurrection of Christ,
in reference to salvation and sin.

Each is related,
and part of the group shot.
It's a group picture,
believe it or not.

God's plan was being worked,
each was part of the play.
From the cross to the grave,
God worked through resurrection day.

This was a group photograph,
God's plan of redemption.
Each part was essential,
and there could be no exemption.

When you look at a group photograph,
think of the death, burial and resurrection.
Then ponder those thoughts,
with serious meditation.

Think of what God did,
to bring you salvation.
It's a group picture.
Receive this revelation.

AUGUST 12

DON'T RUN FROM GOD

God is rich in mercy.
He wants to restore.
Condemnation is not of God,
to you I implore.

Conviction is of God,
and He wants to bless you.
Condemnation is of Satan,
and he wants to destroy you.

Don't run from God,
if you ever blow it.
Run to Him,
and you'll find comfort.

His mind hasn't changed,
towards you.
Believe this truth,
no matter what you do.

If you slip,
He's not there to hit you.
If you slip,
He's there to help you.

Don't run from God.
He loves you so much.
Soften your heart,
and let Him touch.

Towards you,
He has no condemnation.
He wants to give you,
complete restoration.

Receive His mercy.
Come with haste.
Let Him restore you,
and receive His grace.

AUGUST 13

EXAMINE YOUR THOUGHTS

Thoughts are like trains.
They take you somewhere.
Follow the track,
and you'll get there.

Thoughts are like planes.
They take you somewhere.
Follow the route,
and you'll get there.

Thoughts are like buses.
They take you somewhere.
Follow the road,
and you'll get there.

Thoughts have different paths.
Some you shouldn't pursue.
Some are good and some are bad.
Where do your thoughts take you?

Examine your thoughts.
Those that are bad,
oppose the Word of God,
and if followed, will eventually make you sad.

Acts of sin don't just happen.
This is easy to perceive.
Commitment of ill deeds,
are first in thought conceived.

Meditate on an ill pursuit,
and you step onto its path.
Keep walking its way,
and your fate will be cast.

Examine your thoughts.
Where will they take you?
Examine each one,
it's something you should do.

Examine your thoughts.
For those not of God,
don't get on their paths,
and of their ground trod.

Which way does this train go?
Examine its track,
before you get on,
and head for a wreck.

AUGUST 14

COMPOSE A NEW SONG

You can't go back.
What's done is done.
If you live in the past,
then it's time to shun.

It's time to move forward.
Forget the past.
Take your past failures,
and behind you cast.

Don't let them rob you,
and they most certainly will,
of future blessings,
if they linger still.

God forgave you.
Now it's your turn,
to forgive yourself,
and of guilt spurn.

You've asked God's forgiveness,
and He's wiped your slate clean.
So it's time to get on with it,
if you know what I mean.

You heard me right.
You have a clean slate.
Now receive His blessings,
and be bold in faith.

Future blessings await.
Move forward in Christ.
You still have many days,
to live your life.

A bright future is yours,
your past is gone.
With the help of Christ,
you'll compose a new song.

AUGUST 15

TESTIMONY FROM HEAVEN

It's so wonderful here.
The Bible was right.
Heaven is so breathtaking,
with such beautiful sites.

Surrounded by love,
sickness does not exist.
It's such a wonderful place,
I'm glad I didn't miss.

There's no poverty in Heaven,
but abundance always.
It's so much better than earth,
in each and every way.

There's joy unspeakable,
and full of glory.
Peace pervades throughout,
with no signs of worry.

Words cannot describe,
the joy I feel.
Heaven is designed,
with such great appeal.

I say to you,
listen real strong.
Choose to come here,
and you can't go wrong.

The choice is yours.
Jesus gives it to you.
He has prepared a wonderful place,
but you must choose.

Receive His love,
and accept His invitation.
Receive Him as Lord and Savior,
and secure your reservation.

AUGUST 16

TESTIMONY FROM HELL

I lived for the world,
and was not very bright.
Now I'm in Hell,
and it's darker than night.

I'm in great pain here,
and can't ever leave.
Demons continually torment me,
and tell me I was deceived.

Loneliness dwells in me,
and fear is so thick.
Coming to this place,
makes me so sick.

My soul cries for peace,
with gut wrenching cries.
Oh, I lived for the world,
and didn't realize.

I can't go back.
It's now too late.
I'm doomed forever,
with no escape.

I refused to accept Jesus,
and His message of salvation.
I didn't believe,
there was eternal damnation.

The world isn't worth it.
Heed my warning.
If you come here,
you'll have eternal mourning.

The suffering is so great,
and this place is so real.
Accept Jesus as Lord and Savior,
while you have time still.

AUGUST 17

ALIEN

Separated from the world,
He doesn't blend in.
He's a bit peculiar,
if you know what I mean.

He says he's a Christian,
and his home is not here.
He says it's in Heaven,
and later he'll go there.

He's now on assignment,
doing the Lord's work.
He's a considerate fellow,
and one that does not hurt.

Faithful he is,
as he accomplishes his tasks.
He knows things done for God,
are things that will last.

A doer of good,
in this world of turmoil,
he shares the gospel,
all across this earth's soil.

He praises the Lord,
and consistently prays.
He tries to help others,
wherever he may.

He has set his mind,
on things above.
The world and its system,
he does not love.

Yes, he's peculiar,
as he moves among men.
You might consider him,
a visiting alien.

AUGUST 18

AVOID GRASSHOPPER MENTALITY

There are giants in the land.
We saw with our own eyes.
We spied out the land,
and there are men of great size.

There are giants in the land,
and we are so small.
We can't overcome,
for they are so tall.

There are giants in the land.
You must understand,
that we would have to face,
most formidable men.

There are giants in the land.
I wish it were not so.
Defeat awaits,
so we cannot go.

I now warn,
against grasshopper mentality.
For if you're in Christ,
there's a different reality.

Focus on God,
and go in His might.
Stand on His promises,
and don't go by sight.

Giants are real,
in all areas of life,
but you've a different report,
when you're in Christ.

Read God's report.
He says you're able.
When you're in Christ,
you have His label.

Believe His Word,
and speak it out.
Since you're in Christ,
it has great clout.

Speak to that giant,
and he will know,
that since you're in Christ,
he'll have to go.

AUGUST 19

DON'T CRACK THE DOOR

Would you answer your door,
late at night,
and let a murderer in,
right before your sight?

Would you answer your door,
late at night,
and let a thief in,
right before your sight?

Would you answer your door,
late at night,
and let a mugger in,
right before your sight?

The answer is no to all three.
Satan comes to kill, steal and destroy.
Yet people consistently open the door for him,
in ways not coy.

Once the door is cracked,
and you let him in,
then be prepared to reap,
the havoc he sends.

Guard against doubt,
and the approach of fear.
Keep the door shut,
when they come near.

Guard against strife,
and don't let him in.
Guard against unforgiveness,
and any form of sin.

When to your front door,
the devil does come,
resist him well,
and do not succumb.

AUGUST 20

PRISONERS WERE LISTENING

In dungeon and chains,
Paul and Silas were bound.
In spite of it all,
they refused to get down.

Praises came forth,
from out of their hearts,
while other prisoners were listening,
in other cell parts.

It was late at night,
at the midnight hour.
The conditions would've made,
most people sour.

Yet Paul and Silas stood out,
as rays of light,
in the dark dungeon,
late that night.

No matter the conditions,
they would praise the Lord.
No matter how bleak,
they would honor His Word.

As other prisoners listened,
their witness was strong.
The prisoners took notice,
of their praises and song.

Deliverance did come,
during that bleakest of nights,
causing the jailer,
to react with much fright.

The jailer was then saved.
It was an impressive sight,
that was caused by the events,
that took place that night.

Circumstances say one thing,
and are often at odds,
with what the Word says,
and the promises of God.

During adverse circumstances,
what kind of witnesses are we?
Let's keep our eyes on the Word,
that keeps us free.

AUGUST 21

UNITY IN HEART

Nebuchadnezzar had conquered Jerusalem.
Much of Israel was in devastation.
Many Israelites were led off into captivity,
but a time would come for revisitation.

Nehemiah had a saddened heart while in exile.
The King inquired into reasons why.
Nehemiah wanted to return to Jerusalem,
as he responded with sigh.

The King granted Nehemiah's wish.
Nehemiah and others then returned to their homeland.
They proceeded to rebuild Jerusalem's walls and gates,
with great effort required from each man.

The people worked with all their hearts,
as they were threatened with opposition.
Sanballat, Geshem and others plotted against their efforts,
while many Israelites stood guard in their positions.

The wall around Jerusalem was finally completed.
It took an arduous 52 days.
Nehemiah's enemies perceived the Hand of the Lord,
as they saw their self-confidence give way.

Exiles were now free to return.
In the history of Israel this was an important event.
It was accomplished through teamwork and unity,
by Nehemiah and the others sent.

Division works against a church or organization.
On the contrary, unity magnifies its force.
Unity in heart by a group is so important,
that it can dramatically change its course.

To any leader that has an ear,
listen to what I say.
Get your goals into the heart of your people,
and it will pave the way.

AUGUST 22

STATE OF EMERGENCY

People will call 911,
in states of emergency.
They'll often do it,
with great urgency.

Lives have been saved,
from calls that were made,
as medical technicians came,
to render first aid.

Harm has been stopped,
as a result of these calls.
Policemen have come,
for those breaking the law.

These calls are available,
for the physical man.
They're made quite often,
throughout the land.

Many people today,
need to make a call,
in the realm of the spirit,
before curtain call.

God is a spirit,
and He'll send eternal life,
into your spirit,
if you'll accept Jesus Christ.

Recommend go to the phone,
the phone of your heart.
It's time to call,
and do your part.

Call on the Lord,
and He will save you.
Just make the call,
I strongly urge you.

AUGUST 23

TARNISHED BRASS

Tarnished brass looks different,
when it's polished with shine.
Luster is added,
to make it look fine.

The look is different,
although the brass is the same.
In either case,
it's brass by name.

Go to a church service,
during worship and praise.
Observe all the people,
with voices raised.

Some worship has tarnish,
while some has shine.
I respectfully say this,
and don't mean to be unkind.

Some people are reverent,
and have drawn a line,
around them with God,
and have a radiant shine.

Others are daydreaming,
and are going through the motions.
Lip service is there,
without much emotion.

All may be Christians,
and all may be saved,
but of the two groups,
which is the better way?

Worship may be tarnished.
Let's remember this line.
When we worship God,
let's make it shine.

AUGUST 24

OBEDIENCE NETS RESULTS

A fisherman by trade,
he had worked all night.
Peter had caught nothing,
and was tired by sight.

Jesus told him to push out,
and let down his nets.
He proceeded to comply,
and came up with great catch.

Pulling on his nets,
Peter was thoroughly amazed.
He had never seen a catch like this,
in all his days.

Peter's nets began to break,
because they were so filled,
with an abundance of fish,
that brought great thrill.

Obedient to the Lord,
Peter had pushed out.
A message is here,
that one should not doubt.

Obedience is important,
important to the Lord.
Obedience to the Holy Spirit,
will bring great rewards.

If you consent and obey,
you will eat the best of the land.
This scripture is written,
for each receptive man.

Obedience nets results,
so let down your nets.
Launch out with the Lord,
and await your catch.

AUGUST 25

JUDGMENT DADDY

This is a story,
about a man named Freddy.
He often referred to God,
as Judgment Daddy.

Freddy believed God,
was up on a big throne,
waiting to jump on him,
if he did wrong.

Freddy viewed God,
as holding a big stick,
just waiting to beat Freddy,
and give him a good lick.

Then one day,
someone shared some scriptures with Freddy.
He began to realize something different,
about Judgment Daddy.

He began to perceive,
that God actually loved him.
So he began to read more scriptures,
many more of them.

He soon realized,
that God loved him very much.
This started to sink in,
as his heart was touched.

He now knows God,
as one of great compassion.
It's a deep compassion,
not of the world's fashion.

He now knows God,
as one of great mercy,
Who will give living water,
to anyone who's thirsty.

God truly wants to bless.
It's now perfectly clear.
Freddy now views God,
as one so dear.

God is no longer known,
as Judgment Daddy,
but as Loving Father,
to His son Freddy.

AUGUST 26

LOVE GAUGE

A gauge can be used,
to provide a measure.
It can be used for temperature,
or to monitor pressure.

It can be used for testing,
or showing progress.
Data can be obtained,
to improve a process.

The use of gauges,
certainly has mechanical applications,
but in some ways,
use can be applied to human situations.

Take for example love.
Are you walking in love?
This is a commandment,
ordained from above.

Can love be measured?
Is their a way,
to monitor your walk,
from day to day?

An important gauge,
may be used.
You'll quickly know,
if you do.

Do you take account,
of the evil done to you?
The way you react,
tells you if you do.

Don't take account,
but repay evil with good.
It may be hard to do,
but it's something you should.

AUGUST 27

FOUR LEAF CLOVERS

Do you have four leaf clovers,
or a lucky rabbit's foot,
or maybe a horseshoe,
to bring you good luck?

Good luck charms,
are valued possessions,
for people that have,
some real superstitions.

Fear of the unknown,
is released in different ways.
False conceptions of causation,
are still common today.

Can those four leaf clovers,
influence the outcome?
To irrational behavior,
many people succumb.

Trust is important,
when it's in the right place.
Now at this point,
I'll talk of God's grace.

Look to God's Word,
for it is true.
It's all you need,
to pull you through.

As you trust in God,
you'll receive divine intervention.
It's much more reliable,
than some blind superstition.

Trust in God.
He wants to help you.
In all areas of your life,
He wants to bless you.

AUGUST 28

YES-MAN

He's known as Yes-man.
He got his name,
by always agreeing with the boss,
on all subjects same.

He stifles his opinions,
and keeps them shut in.
Everything has his approval,
he's always willing to bend.

No disagreement here,
or constructive words.
He's known as Yes-man,
as you've just heard.

He doesn't rock the boat,
not this man.
He tries to always get along,
as much as he can.

To Christians I ask,
in reference to sin,
are you like Yes-man,
and always willing to bend?

As sin occurs around you,
do you always condone?
Do you always agree with the group,
and never stand out alone?

Do you stand up for what's right,
or just blend in?
How do you react,
when confronted with sin?

Your walk is important.
God is now prompting you.
It's more important to please Him,
in all you say and do.

AUGUST 29

FATE OF THE DRAGON

The dragon hates God,
let it be known.
He has ever since,
he was cast from God's throne.

In the image of God,
man was made.
This helps explain,
why traps are laid.

He'll do what he can,
to destroy each man.
He'll try and interfere,
with God's redemption plan.

Destruction of lives,
the dragon aggressively pursues.
Sly schemes are devised,
and then they're used.

The dragon breathes fire,
along his destructive path.
He thinks he can win,
but his fate is cast.

His time is short,
it's coming near.
These are words,
he doesn't want to hear.

His future is sealed,
and it's not very bright.
It's like his day is passing,
and it'll soon be night.

To the Lake of Fire,
the dragon will be cast.
He'll be there forever,
throughout years that last.

AUGUST 30

IF CLAUSE

The promises of God,
are wonderful indeed,
but conditions are there,
that you must heed.

Check God's promises,
and when you do,
you'll see this process,
to be so true.

If you do this,
then you'll get that.
After you look at a promise,
then check its track.

You'll often see,
a certain stipulation.
When this occurs,
then you must meet that condition.

The promises are there,
and are certainly yours,
but you must meet conditions,
and properly adhere.

If results don't come,
perhaps you didn't qualify.
Were conditions met,
and did you comply?

God always honors His Word.
The problem is not Him.
Each promise He honors,
each and every one of them.

Check your walk,
and if adjustments are required.
Then freely make them,
and stand for what's desired.

AUGUST 31

PITY PARTY

Are you feeling down,
because someone did you wrong?
Are you feeling down,
because you heard a sad song?

Set the stage,
and put the light on you.
In a theatrical way,
it's what you do.

The play is set to begin.
Give selfishness his cue.
It's his time on stage,
as he comes out of you.

This play does have,
such self-centered acts.
Let the pity out,
and don't hold back.

So something didn't work out,
and now you're sad.
The Lord would say,
it's time to get glad.

Through the Blood of Jesus,
God has made you righteous.
So proclaim the Word,
for you've been made victorious.

No problem is too great,
that God can't turn around.
It's time to be strong,
and hold your ground.

Trust in the Lord,
to be your strong right hand.
He can handle any problem,
that's common to man.

SEPTEMBER 1

TALK ABOUT JEWELS

Many people get excited,
about nice diamond rings.
Many people get excited,
about rubies, sapphires and other things.

Jewels have an attraction,
that holds many eyes.
Many are truly attractive,
of this I won't deny.

If you're attracted to jewels,
and the beauty they show,
then let's take a trip,
and to Revelations we'll go.

Let's look at some jewels.
and visit this place,
that will blow your mind,
with its walls and gates.

Take a look at the New Jerusalem.
Take a look at its walls.
Look at all the foundations,
look at them all.

Precious stones will be seen,
of brilliance so great.
Then take a look at the pearls,
that compose each gate.

Now cast your eyes,
at the streets of pure gold.
The splendor is great,
as the Bible foretold.

You'll be able to come,
if you're in the Lamb's Book of Life.
To get your name listed,
then accept Jesus Christ.

SEPTEMBER 2

NO MORE LEDGER

Get out the ledger,
and grab the pen.
There's something else,
that can now be entered in.

Nasty words were said,
that were certainly heard.
Time to write them down,
the words that were heard.

Another entry made,
and recorded well.
It will be viewed again,
as time will tell.

Other entries have been made,
in similar style.
They've all been recorded,
and placed on file.

The memory is good,
and retrieves them well.
It will even take time,
and on them dwell.

It's now the time,
to be politely curt.
It isn't God's way,
to record these hurts.

Forgive and forget,
just let them go.
For if you don't,
they again will show.

Let them go.
It's best for you.
God will tell you,
it's what you should do.

SEPTEMBER 3

MANY REASONS BUT NO EXCUSE

Look at that Bible,
sitting on the table.
You say you'll pick it up,
when you're able.

You've had a long week,
and now it's the weekend.
Things are planned for Saturday,
and on Sunday you must rest in.

The day was real busy,
and you were going to pray,
but now it's so late,
and at the end of the day.

You were going to the prayer meeting,
but there's a special on tonight.
Maybe you'll go next week,
or on some other night.

You were going to tithe,
but funds are short.
Maybe next year,
you'll have a better report.

Help is needed at church,
but you just don't have time.
You're not able to help out,
but hope things work out fine.

Your neighbor needs the Lord,
but you don't want to offend.
You hope someone else will minister,
and help save her from sin.

A Christian brother is in the hospital,
and you were going to visit,
but something came up,
and you just had to forget it.

Many reasons exist,
that sound good to the mind,
but there's really no excuse,
most of the time.

Set your mind on things above,
and not on this earth.
That's what the Lord says,
after you've received the new birth.

SEPTEMBER 4

STAND GUARD WITH THE BLOOD

Soldiers must stand guard,
during times of war.
Against the enemy,
they must not open doors.

Standing guard requires diligent effort.
This is a time of watchfulness,
for the enemy will take advantage,
of any neglect or carelessness.

The enemy looks for openings,
as he seeks destruction.
Attacks will be made,
if there is no obstruction.

Christians are in war.
They are under reconnaissance.
Their enemy never sleeps,
as he maintains constant surveillance.

To a slothful Christian,
much is at stake,
for the enemy will take advantage,
of any costly mistakes.

Watchfulness is important to victory.
It never ends.
A Christian must continually watch,
if he is to defend.

No Christian is excused.
Christians are not to be overcome.
They are to triumph in Christ,
and of defeat not succumb.

Christians must be vigilant.
Their strength is in Christ,
and the power of His Blood,
that protects their lives.

Christians should daily apply the Blood.
It will serve them well,
against the wiles of the enemy,
and of his assaults repel.

Pleading the Blood of Jesus,
must be common place,
for the born again Christian,
saved by God's grace.

SEPTEMBER 5

FRAGILITY OF LIFE

A car just missed a stoplight,
and hit a teenage girl.
The young girl just died,
and left this world.

A few minutes ago,
she never imagined this,
but now life is gone,
and it doesn't exist.

A few minutes ago,
she was full of life,
but now I ponder,
was she in Christ.

I expect she had plans,
for a life ahead,
but those plans are gone,
for she's now dead.

What matters most,
was she in Christ.
One must receive Him,
while there is life.

Your plans may be important,
but when you leave this world,
you'll leave them behind,
just like this young girl.

If you had an accident,
like this young girl,
where would you be,
if you left this world?

There's fragility in life,
death is just a heartbeat away.
If you haven't received Christ,
then receive Him today.

<u>SEPTEMBER 6</u>

TAKE A GOOD LOOK

Nebuchadnezzar, look in the fire,
what do you see?
Take a good look,
when you look at the three.

You see a fourth man,
walking among the three.
He's like a Son of God,
it's clear as can be.

They're in the fire,
but have supernatural protection.
Now you see why,
they gave you rejection.

There's a superior being,
and He's not you.
It's something the three,
already knew.

What do you think,
time to change your opinion?
Your attitude now seems different,
not full of rebellion.

Two points immediately come out,
when one looks at this scene.
As one looks closely,
one will glean.

God is committed to you,
as you trust in Him,
and if you doubt He exists,
it's time to accept Him.

If you're in Jesus,
then He goes with you,
no matter where you go,
no matter what you do.

<u>SEPTEMBER 7</u>

HIT THE DEVIL

A fighter is jarred,
when in the ring,
if he gets hit,
with a punch that stings.

When a fighter connects,
with a stiff left hook,
it'll jar his opponent,
and affect his look.

The physical force,
of a strong right hand,
will make an impression,
when it lands.

Now open your eyes,
to the other world,
and on this theme,
sit and twirl.

Watch the devil,
when he is punched,
with the Word of God,
that hits with crunch.

Notice his expression,
and the pain he feels.
The Word to him,
is a bitter pill.

Notice his eyes,
and how they roll.
Time to leave,
for some other soul.

You hit him hard,
and made him flee.
You've used the weapon,
that makes him leave.

SEPTEMBER 8

RESIST THE FLEAS

A dog with fleas,
will scratch with paw.
Sometimes his skin,
will even become raw.

The fleas bite,
and serve as pests.
They'll even lay eggs,
and attempt to nest.

Lay down with the devil,
and you'll get fleas.
Of his influence,
do not receive.

In your daily walk,
watch out for his fleas.
You must resist them,
if you want to remain free.

They'll hop with speed,
and try to lay hold,
to your very mind,
and very soul.

There's the flea of doubt,
and the flea of fear.
There's the flea of worry,
who'll try and stay real near.

Other fleas come from the devil,
that are very real.
Again, I say to you,
to them not yield.

You must resist the devil,
and give him the Word.
You must resist the devil,
and stand on God's Word.

SEPTEMBER 9

WHITE HOT

It's time to ask,
about your spiritual mettle.
Is it white hot,
like molten metal?

Do you ever think,
about your eternal life,
or about your heavenly future,
that will be so nice?

Do the things of the world,
hold you in grip,
as you hold carnal desires,
and won't let them slip?

Are you concerned for souls,
and their eternal destination,
or does this subject,
just provide mere fascination?

Are you drawn to the Word,
and the promises therein,
or are you nonchalant,
about the contents within?

Are praise, prayer and worship,
important to you,
or maybe they don't really fit,
in what you do?

These are days,
to be white hot.
These aren't days,
to be not.

Get on fire,
and stoke the coals.
Heat up your mettle,
with eternal goals.

SEPTEMBER 10

GIVE AN ACCOUNT

Will the next Christian,
proceed to the Judgment Seat?
The angel is maintaining order,
and keeping things neat.

Prepare your thoughts,
for you must give an account,
for all your days,
no matter the count.

You're now before God.
His eyes are on you,
as He examines your life,
and inquires of you.

Were you a good servant,
or did you waste your days?
Truth will be known,
since you're under God's gaze.

Did you run your race,
with a banner for Christ,
or were you indifferent,
throughout your life?

Did you seek His kingdom,
in the things you did,
or follow your own pursuits,
and of Christ's hid?

Time has run out,
no time to go back.
It'll be too late,
if your life shows lack.

Your time is now.
It's on earth you act.
It's here you make sure,
that your life won't lack.

SEPTEMBER 11

WHITE THRONE JUDGMENT

Will the next person,
proceed to the White Throne?
You're next in line,
and cannot roam.

You conned many people,
and to many lied.
It's time to con God,
now that you've died.

Better think quickly,
you're good at that.
You did it on earth,
with quite a knack.

Think of an excuse,
and sell it well.
Make sure it's good,
to get out of Hell.

You were going to accept Jesus,
later in life,
but you were too busy,
to receive Christ.

It didn't seem important,
during the days of your life,
but things are now different,
concerning salvation and Christ.

You've changed your mind,
and now want to receive salvation.
There's no need,
for eternal damnation.

God has just pointed,
from the White Throne,
to the flames of Hell,
that'll be your eternal home.

It'll be a tragic sight,
a terrible scene,
if you're that one,
in this scene.

It's time to wake up,
this isn't a lie.
You must receive Jesus,
before you die.

SEPTEMBER 12

HOW'S YOUR WARDROBE

Open up your clothes closet,
and take a look inside.
You'll should find certain items,
that should be set side by side.

Take your hat of salvation,
and put it on your head.
You're now alive in God,
and no longer dead.

Take your shirt of righteousness,
and put it on neatly from place.
Money couldn't buy it,
for it was given by God's grace.

Take your pants of joy,
and wear them against sadness.
You've victory in God,
and have no room for bitterness.

Take your belt of truth,
and place it around your waist.
You'll know the devil's lies,
as he tries to make his case.

Take your shoes of gospel peace,
and fit them on your feet.
Share the gospel with others,
so they can have victory and not defeat.

Take your coat of faith,
and wear it well.
It's the opposite of fear,
that so bothers Hell.

Take the ring of God's promises,
and wear them on your hand.
Speak them against the enemy,
as you possess your land.

SEPTEMBER 13

BENEFITS

People often seek,
benefits in an occupation.
You know this is true,
throughout the nation.

Benefits are important,
let's be real.
So let's look at something,
that'll bring great thrill.

This isn't an occupation,
but it'll change your life.
It'll bring great benefits,
if you accept Jesus Christ.

First, when you accept Jesus,
you receive eternal life,
with a home in Heaven,
that is much greater than nice.

Next, other blessings are available,
when you receive salvation.
Wonderful blessings are yours,
if you'll receive this revelation.

Whatever you need,
is in Jesus' Name.
Many promises are available,
if you'll lay claim.

You've been redeemed,
when you accept Jesus Christ,
from the curse of the law,
and all its strife.

Blessings are yours,
starting in this earthly realm.
So receive benefits now,
there are many of them.

<u>SEPTEMBER 14</u>

GOD IS ABLE AND WILLING

God is great,
and He is capable,
of performing great deeds,
for He is able.

God parted the Red Sea,
and safely delivered the Israelites.
It was a mighty deed,
a colossal sight.

A fourth in the furnace,
Nebuchadnezzar saw,
as the three others,
were protected from all.

Hungry lions wouldn't attack Daniel,
down in the lions' den.
An angel stood guard,
that God did send.

God watched over David,
as David hurled his stone,
and before Goliath knew it,
his life was gone.

Ten lepers departed Jesus,
healed from their disease.
Health was restored,
as they were all pleased.

Jesus took the loaves and fishes,
and effected great change,
to feed the multitude,
that to hear Him came.

Payment for sins,
was made at the cross,
because of God's love,
for all the lost.

Whatever you need,
God is able.
Trust in Him,
for He is capable.

Look in the Bible,
it is His will.
Locate the promise,
that will seal your deal.

<u>SEPTEMBER 15</u>

BOLD ACCESS

The word bold,
portrays a picture of fearlessness.
The word bold,
isn't a word you caress.

It has a distinct quality,
that conveys an intrepid spirit.
It brings up qualities,
of fortitude and endurance.

God says to Christians,
to come boldly before His throne.
That means with confidence and assurance,
and not with faces sad and long.

What an impressive thought.
Christians have bold access to the Father,
and He wants Christians to come,
for they're never a bother.

Come boldly to the throne,
for your loving Father awaits.
It's through the name of Jesus,
that you open its gates.

Don't be apprehensive,
or come in fear,
but come with confidence and reverence,
when you draw near.

Never dread coming to the Father,
a father of great love,
when you petition His throne,
and send prayers above.

Come boldly to His throne,
for you have direct access.
Come boldly with concerns,
the Word does attest.

SEPTEMBER 16

A FATHER'S LOVE

Her voice speaks softly,
"Daddy, wait for me."
So Daddy slows up,
as she tugs at his knee.

Her little hand reaches up,
to grab at her father's hand.
He then bends down and touches her,
as only he can.

A twinkle comes to his eyes,
as he looks upon her face,
words are not needed,
nor is there haste.

There's a certain love,
deep within his heart,
embedded with joy,
never to depart.

Nothing could take that love.
It's worth more than silver or gold.
It's part of him,
and never could be sold.

Her life is of more value,
than his very own.
He'll sacrifice his life,
trying to provide her a good home.

He's made in the image of God,
oh, can it be,
just ask his little girl,
and then you'll see.

SEPTEMBER 17

FORWARD PRESENCE

Forward presence of military units,
demonstrates national resolve.
It strengthens alliances,
and dissuades adversary involvement.

It enhances a country's ability,
to respond to contingency operations.
Forward presence of military units,
promotes the security of nations.

In the lives of Christians,
a forward presence exists,
of God's mighty angels,
innumerable to list.

Angels beckon to God's call,
to oppose the adversary,
to serve God's children,
when it is necessary.

Projected on earth,
this is a forward presence,
prepared for conflict,
that has been Heaven sent.

Maintaining their stations,
they are faithful and true,
to carry out God's orders,
in all they do.

So in life's battles,
never forget,
that there's a forward presence,
when you're in the thick of it.

God's angels are forward deployed,
and they'll watch over you.
Just proclaim and trust in God's Word,
and He'll see you through.

SEPTEMBER 18

UNCONTROLLED ANGER

Anger is not necessarily sin.
Uncontrolled it is sinful and can cause devastation.
Controlled it can be used for good,
and diverted to zeal while avoiding transgression.

The Bible says a fool loses his temper,
but a wise man holds it back.
An angry man will stir up strife,
with a quite a knack.

Uncontrolled anger is to be put away,
for it will show deeds of the flesh.
Uncontrolled anger counteracts peace,
and with it will not mesh.

Uncontrolled anger shatters relationships,
and can lead to frustration and depression.
Peace must be sought after bouts of uncontrolled anger,
to preclude unreconciliation.

A believer given to uncontrolled anger demonstrates,
that he is in fact out of control,
and that he is focusing on things passing in time,
while playing a foolish and sinful role.

A believer thus shows that he is reacting,
and that his rights are not yielded to Christ.
He is defending himself,
which can place him in a selfish light.

Uncontrolled anger must be confronted,
it must not be excused.
It is sin and not pleasing to God,
and will cause one to ultimately lose.

Confess it as sin,
and renew your mind as you put on the new man.
Don't let emotions or feelings activate your responses,
and learn to think in the ways of God as you take your stand.

SEPTEMBER 19

THE BIBLE

There is one source book,
for the Christian's daily walk.
It's the Bible,
of which I talk.

It's inspired by God,
and profitable for teaching.
It's also profitable for reproof and correction,
and even righteous training.

Valuable guidance is in the Bible,
and certainly comes forth,
for man to refer to,
and steer his course.

Change is a continuing theme,
that certainly is found,
and if one is receptive,
one will be on solid ground.

Change is expected,
and commanded by the Bible.
Salvation is the first step,
towards one's spiritual revival.

Change is a growing process,
continual and not automatic.
A believer must then move forward,
and not remain static.

Progress will be seen,
as the Bible is studied and received,
as the scriptures are acted upon,
and within the heart believed.

The Bible is a life changing book.
It affects behavior, speech, attitudes, and thinking,
not to mention eternal salvation,
and motives for living.

SEPTEMBER 20

FRESH MANNA

The Israelites daily ate fresh manna.
Fresh manna is still important today,
for a born again Christian,
who wants to follow God's way.

It's in the form of the Word,
that I refer to fresh manna today.
The Christian must consume the Word,
and do it each and every day.

The Word must be fresh,
so it can generate fresh fire.
The Word must be fresh,
so it can generate Godly desires.

The Word must be fresh,
so it can generate fresh vision.
The Word must be fresh,
so it can cause Godly decisions.

The Word must be fresh,
so it can generate fresh vigor,
The Word must be fresh,
so it can rejuvenate against life's rigors.

The Word must be fresh,
so it can restore peace.
The Word must be fresh,
so that worry will cease.

The Word must be fresh,
so that joy comes back.
The Word must be fresh,
so that one doesn't lack.

The Word must be received and believed,
as from the heart of Christ.
The Word must be received and believed,
allowing it to generate new life.

SEPTEMBER 21

TRUE FRIEND

Many folks,
and some even close,
will tell you what you want to hear,
as they serve as obliging hosts.

These folks,
don't want to offend,
and are only trying to be nice,
whether it be relatives or friends.

You may feel good,
as you receive these replies,
but in many cases,
they may be small lies.

It has been said,
that true friends,
will tell you the truth,
even if it offends.

Truth is important,
and will be to your gain.
It may sting at first,
but it can save you much pain.

No games involved,
or delusions of self,
for truth always comes,
from the correct shelf.

It's in your best interest,
to receive truth from a friend,
even at times,
if it does offend.

That's why the Bible,
is your truest of friends,
for it always steers you,
away from the destructions of sin.

SEPTEMBER 22

TEACH YOUR CHILDREN

Parents have responsibilities,
when they bring children into this world.
They must teach them things,
that apply to both boys and girls.

They must teach them to love God,
and serve Him in spirit and truth.
They must teach principles of faith,
and confront teachings of untruth.

They must teach them biblical love,
in a world surrounded by hate.
They must encourage and support,
and with their time obligate.

They must teach them to obey,
and honor the Word and laws of the land.
They must teach them good work ethics,
and guide them towards integrity and honest stands.

They must teach biblical forgiveness,
and personal responsibility.
They must teach effective communication,
and biblical morality.

They must teach them to choose good friends,
and what to look for in a good mate.
They must teach them to make good decisions,
in order to preclude later mistakes.

Parents must not leave their child's training,
to just anyone and everyone.
Parents have personal responsibilities,
to their daughters or sons.

Adults are in prisons,
throughout many lands,
because their parents never taught them about living,
in accordance with God's plan.

SEPTEMBER 23

CHANGE

It's very interesting,
to observe a Christian's face.
His reaction to gospel teaching,
can often be traced.

Talk about healing,
or perhaps on prosperity,
and you'll get favorable reactions,
with great regularity.

Talk about benefits,
and the promises of the Lord,
and you'll often prevent people,
from getting bored.

Now shift the subjects,
and talk about change,
and many reactions,
will not be the same.

Tell the people,
that they need to change,
and some may wonder,
why they came.

You see time and effort,
are often involved,
in the process of change,
to help one evolve.

Not a favorite subject,
it's one of great importance,
for change is important,
to develop one's substance.

People can't develop,
and go further in God's plan,
if they're not willing to change,
under the instruction of God's hand.

SEPTEMBER 24

PROPER COMMUNICATION

Proper communication is important,
and is essential to growth and fellowship.
Its effects can be seen in the spiritual and physical realms,
and in all areas of relationships.

Unbiblical communication often generates,
a path of destructiveness,
in the lives of family, friends and associates,
which leads to lives of brokenness.

Listening is so important,
and must not be treated irreverently,
People must focus on true meaning and intent,
and avoid responding too quickly.

Bitterness in heart,
produces bitterness of speech.
Avoiding critical and judgmental attitudes,
is worthwhile to teach.

Speaking the truth is important,
and should be done with kindness.
Problems must be discussed,
but not with resentment and bitterness.

Don't hold anger overnight,
and allow it to linger.
Deal with the problem soonest,
when it begins to build anger.

Attack the problem, not the person,
and look for a solution.
This is much more constructive,
while seeking resolution.

Act in love and don't negatively react.
Don't react with argumentative bitterness,
but take the biblical path,
and act in kindness and forgiveness.

SEPTEMBER 25

FLIP THE SWITCH

Flip the switch,
on your wall.
It didn't take,
much time at all.

Now consider a life span,
of maybe 80 years.
Listen closely,
with your ears.

That flip of the switch,
takes more time,
than the span of your life,
when compared to all time.

Your span of life,
is almost nothing at all,
and can be compared,
to the switch on the wall.

Your eternal years,
beyond the grave,
will far outlast,
your current days.

These few years on earth,
will affect your eternal destiny.
To live for the world,
will be a form of blasphemy.

Common sense does say,
to get on fire,
and serve the Lord God,
with the strongest desire.

Flip the switch of your priorities,
and flip it for good.
Serve the Lord well,
as you know you should.

SEPTEMBER 26

POWER PROJECTION

Power projection is a military term.
It projects an offensive military thrust,
against an enemy at a chosen place and time,
and involves elements of force.

Power projection is designed,
to take the offensive.
It's designed towards victory,
and to be aggressive.

Christian soldiers know of this strategy,
and use it in a similar way.
They regularly practice it,
when they pray.

You see prayer is designed in a comparable manner,
to take the offensive.
It projects a force against the enemy,
and can be very aggressive.

It targets the enemy,
and is designed to destroy,
the works of the enemy,
and the schemes he employs.

Land is taken back,
as victory is seized,
because some praying saints,
got down on their knees.

In military terms,
power projection is important.
In Christian terms,
power projection is equally important.

The enemy is real,
so take the offensive.
Destroy his works in prayer,
and become aggressive.

SEPTEMBER 27

JOB OPPORTUNITIES AVAILABLE

Job opportunities are available.
There's no shortage of jobs.
No need to stand in line,
or behind a large mob.

Applications are taken,
if you want to apply.
There's work for all,
with no need to deny.

Assistance in church,
is one area of need.
Listen to church announcements,
and do take heed.

To the ministry of helps,
all are called.
Everyone gets,
to play with this ball.

The necessity of prayer,
should get attention.
It must be stressed,
and not merely mentioned.

Witnessing for Jesus,
or passing out tracts,
is clearly an area,
that should not lack.

Job opportunities are available.
There's no shortage of jobs.
No need to stand in line,
or behind a large mob.

It's simple to apply,
and easy to start.
All it takes,
is a willing heart.

SEPTEMBER 28

AUTUMN LEAVES

The breezes are cooler,
and there's a change in the air.
The leaves are changing colors,
for autumn is near.

The baton is being passed,
from summer to fall.
Each is reacting,
to nature's call.

Change is coming,
if you take a look.
It's all planned out,
in nature's book.

Now open your eyes,
and take a look,
of changes cited,
in God's Book.

The leaves are changing,
in the annals of time.
Breezes have increased,
and brought in signs.

The fig tree has budded,
and knowledge has increased.
Now take a look at violence,
in the streets.

Disasters have increased,
with a rising pulse.
This isn't a game,
or some kind of hoax.

Yes, open your eyes,
and read God's Book.
Changes are cited,
if you take a look.

Prepare to meet Jesus,
it'll be real soon.
If you're in Christ,
there'll be no gloom.

For those in Christ,
it'll be a great day.
For those without Him,
then they'll have to stay.

SEPTEMBER 29

WHAT'S THAT IN YOUR HAND?

When one works,
one is rewarded.
One gets a paycheck,
for services rendered.

When one sins,
one is rewarded.
One gets a paycheck,
for services rendered.

The reward of work,
is monetary restitution.
The reward of sin,
is insidious destruction.

Sin may disguise itself,
in bright colors of fun,
but the colors will fade,
and then there'll be none.

Sin is a tough employer.
It gives no breaks.
To you it'll harm,
when you take its bait.

The price is too great,
to be on its payroll.
You'll feel the effects,
in your body, spirit and soul.

Sin's paycheck will be issued,
rather you like it or not.
To the one it's issued,
there'll be problems fraught.

What's that in your hand?
Is it a paycheck?
Know how you got it,
and of my words not neglect.

<u>SEPTEMBER 30</u>

KEEP OUT

To keep out intruders,
no trespassing signs are often seen.
Posted along fences,
you're see them around many scenes.

Bold letters "Keep Out",
make a clear statement,
to preclude entry,
and signal curtailment.

To your mind,
I will say this.
Intruders will try and gain entry,
and sometimes persist.

Don't let them in.
To the intruder of doubt,
tell him he's not welcome,
and he has to get out.

Do the same to his friend.
To the intruder of fear,
tell him to be gone,
for he's not welcome here.

When you stand on the promises of God,
these two intruders will try and get in.
Refuse to accept them,
and refuse to bend.

Doubt and fear are designed,
to rob you of faith.
They cause vain imaginations,
and of your confidence will take.

Post "Keep Out" signs,
to doubt and fear.
Resist in the name of Jesus,
and make it very clear.

<u>OCTOBER 1</u>

CHOSEN INSTRUMENT

How could it be,
but it is so.
That's why Ananias,
you must go.

Go talk to Saul,
it is my will.
You must pray for him,
even if not thrilled.

He's a chosen instrument,
and he will change.
From this point on,
he won't be the same.

Saul persecuted Christians,
with much shame,
but now he will turn,
and do great things.

He's a chosen instrument,
and will influence others,
to come to Christ,
and become Christian brothers.

So it is,
with many in darkness,
before they receive light,
and become righteous.

Each Christian has a work,
in the kingdom of God.
It's at this point,
that I will prod.

Wherever you're placed,
shed the light.
You're a chosen instrument,
so others can receive sight.

OCTOBER 2

WALK IN LOVE

Keep the flesh under,
and walk in love.
It has been ordained,
from Heaven above.

Love endures long,
and is patient and kind,
walking in love,
is totally in line.

Love is not arrogant or rude,
nor envious or jealous.
It doesn't hold grudges,
or retain malice.

It believes the best in others,
and is not touchy or fretful.
It doesn't fail,
and is never hateful.

It is not self-seeking,
with carnal talk,
but is concerned for others,
in a Christian's walk.

Walking in love,
shows God to all.
It's a powerful force,
that has a strong call.

People will be touched,
by this wonderful force,
and will look more deeply,
seeking its source.

Be set free,
and follow God's plan.
You'll help others,
and be the better man.

OCTOBER 3

SMALL DEBTS

A man was forgiven,
of a great dollar debt,
but wouldn't forgive another,
and attempted to collect.

A small fee it was,
just a slight amount,
but the other couldn't pay,
as tensions did mount.

Action was taken,
and to prison was sent,
this unfortunate other,
who owed such a small pittance.

Not pleasing to the man,
who forgave the big debt,
the first man was now thrown into prison,
until his payment was met.

A lesson is here,
and must be gleaned,
as we look more closely,
at this scene.

God forgives each of us,
of an enormous debt,
but what about others,
when against we set.

To hold grudges,
and not to forgive,
the smallest of things,
and in bitterness live.

This isn't God's way,
so we must forgive,
all those small debts,
as long as we live.

OCTOBER 4

DISOBEDIENCE

A Christian in disobedience,
must confront and deal with it.
The first step in this process,
is before God to repent.

He then proceeds,
unto God to confess,
and ask for forgiveness,
in the next step of process.

Obedience is appropriate,
now that he's forgiven.
He must be obedient,
and demonstrate proper living.

Disobedience affects divine fellowship,
and it's something to avoid.
It'll affect one's walk,
and create an uneasy void.

Disobedience must be dealt with,
or it will harden one's heart.
That's why the Holy Spirit prompts one,
to repent, confess and do their part.

Deal with disobedience,
it's truly the best way.
Get right with the Lord,
this very day.

God will forgive,
if a Christian will ask.
It's because of the cross,
and a love that lasts.

God loves us so,
and wants complete restoration.
This is a message that pertains,
to all of us Christians.

OCTOBER 5

SAVE THE WHALES

Save the environment,
or save the whales.
You may hear this at rallies,
as many people yell.

Save the spotted owl,
or keep the oceans clean.
People can get real excited,
and even mean.

Many become fervent,
about causes like this.
Many want to protect,
the endangered list.

Fervency is noted,
and energy is spent.
Many protest,
with good intent.

These concerns may be important,
but so are men's souls.
Wouldn't it be great,
to make man top goal?

Man has an eternal spirit,
and is of supreme importance to God.
If you're familiar with the Bible,
then there should be favorable nod.

The earth is passing,
and Armageddon will come.
Souls are perishing,
while many remain mum.

It's time to spread the gospel,
and help save mankind.
It's time for us all,
to get priorities in line.

OCTOBER 6

BE A BLESSING

You should be a blessing.
This may sound trite,
but it's the way to be,
if you want to be right.

As you bless others,
you will certainly be blessed.
You reap what you sow,
is what God attests.

As you look around,
you'll see plenty of needs.
So be a blessing,
and perform good deeds.

Encourage others,
and be quick to send,
gestures of goodwill,
and with love extend.

A friendly word here,
and a smile there,
will often go far,
to showing you care.

Resources and time,
may be required,
to help others,
become unmired.

You can't take it with you,
so the phrase goes,
so be a blessing,
as I've proposed.

God won't forget,
and neither will they,
the ones you've helped,
when it comes Judgment Day.

OCTOBER 7

PEARLS

Many don't agree,
with the gospel story.
Many will deny,
its wonderful glory.

Many will refuse,
and scoff and knock.
Many will insult,
and callously mock.

It's a privilege to hear,
but they don't realize,
its wonderful value,
as you might surmise.

Perceive its beauty,
and its great value too,
and see how it equates,
to pearls so true.

Sometimes it's wise,
to hold your pearls in hand.
Not all are receptive,
in totality of man.

Be led of the Spirit,
is best to say,
as you deal with man,
from day to day.

The Spirit knows,
the heart of each man.
The Spirit knows,
which way it bends.

Be led of the Spirit,
and cast on go,
but hold in hand,
when the leading's no.

OCTOBER 8

MOST THOROUGHLY IMAGINATIVE

Walking near a forest,
I spied on a squirrel.
This prompted me to consider,
all the creatures of the world.

I thought of the giraffe,
and then the rhinoceros.
I thought of the leopard,
and then the hippopotamus.

I thought of the elephant,
and then the tiger.
I thought of the dolphin,
and then the otter.

I thought of the rabbit,
and then the bear.
I thought of the wolf,
and then the deer.

I thought of the dog,
and common cat.
I thought of the cow,
and flying bat.

Then there were the birds,
to add to the list,
not to mention,
all types of fish.

It's hard to fathom,
all the species and types,
that exist on this planet,
as hard as you might.

I came to this conclusion.
God is certainly creative,
and in the truest of sense,
most thoroughly imaginative.

OCTOBER 9

MEDITATION AND MEDICATION

The doctor prescribes medication,
to combat physical ills.
Sometimes it's done,
in the form of pills.

If properly taken,
one should physically improve,
but always the first step,
is from the package remove.

Check expiration dates,
as you know you should.
It needs to be fresh,
for you want it to do good.

Medication not taken,
will in no way assist.
If not taken,
benefits are missed.

Pause for a moment,
and consider biblical meditation.
Now compare this,
to prescribed medication.

Benefits are derived,
from biblical meditation,
much in the same manner,
as prescribed medication.

Make sure the meditation is fresh,
for it will greatly assist,
towards fulfillment of promises,
that you don't want to miss.

Quality time of this nature,
spent in biblical meditation,
should be considered as important,
as that of prize medication.

OCTOBER 10

WORLD WAS FRAMED

The world was framed,
through the use of words.
Perhaps this surprises you,
or maybe you've heard.

There's a detailed account,
of which I'll give reference.
It's the primary source,
that must have preference.

The account I speak of,
is located in the Bible.
After reading the account,
there can be no denial.

Turn to Genesis Chapter One,
and you'll see that when God spoke,
the world came into being,
this isn't a hoax.

God wants you to know,
that when you received salvation,
you received His Spirit,
which is great revelation.

The same Spirit of God,
that spoke the world into being,
now dwells in you,
it's logical reasoning.

Since this is true,
consider your words,
based on the story,
that you've just heard.

Your words have an affect,
on things around you.
Use them wisely,
in all you do.

OCTOBER 11

DOGFIGHT

Picture yourself,
up in the sky.
You're in a fighter aircraft,
and you're up real high.

You're in a dogfight,
with another plane.
A little later on,
I'll reveal its name.

Check to the left,
and check to the right.
Keep your eyes open,
and maintain keen sight.

Maintain your watch,
and keep your mind clear.
As you stay on guard,
and retain good steer.

You and your aircraft,
are in reality one.
You get special directions,
from God's Son.

The other aircraft,
it's also part of you,
but it's the part,
you must renew.

Your spirit and soul,
continuously wage this war.
It's in your mind,
where they fight for score.

To help your spirit win,
renew your soul.
You renew with the Word of God,
advice that will never grow old.

OCTOBER 12

KEEP YOUR SHOUT

The enemy will come,
and try to get your shout.
Any Christian living,
knows what I'm talking about.

He'll come with apathy,
and try to take it away.
A Christian must repel it,
and not give sway.

He may try other things,
such as depression.
A Christian must resist it,
and not accept this oppression.

If that doesn't work,
he may try rebellion.
It was this very sin,
that got him kicked out of Heaven.

Whatever the scheme,
don't lose your shout.
From the words of your lips,
only let victory come out.

I say it again,
don't lose your shout.
It'll affect your confession,
and bring seeds of doubt.

Even if you don't feel like it,
shout anyway.
Keep your shout,
come what may.

Keep your shout strong,
and victory lay claim.
Remember things in the temporal,
are subject to change.

OCTOBER 13

CLOTHES OF APATHY

Too many Christians,
in America today,
just move along,
without much to say.

Things don't matter,
or who really cares,
is a common theme,
that should make Christians beware.

God said to pray,
and He would hear.
He would heal their land,
their land so dear.

Things will change,
if Christians will pray.
Repent and pray,
to effect change this day.

It's time for the church,
to change its clothes.
It's time for the church,
to chase demonic foes.

Take off clothes of apathy,
and put on clothes of concern.
It's time to pursue purpose,
and of right change discern.

Let go of apathy,
your prayers do count.
It's time to pray,
with steadfast amounts.

Prayer is important.
The devil surely knows,
that as you get serious,
it will cause him woe.

Change will take place,
if Christians will take heed,
in the business of God,
with prayerful lead.

Let go of apathy,
and do your part.
Get busy in prayer,
and let it come from your heart.

OCTOBER 14

PUT A SMILE ON YOUR FACE

Check out faces,
when you attend church.
Simply by observing,
you'll see much.

Some will smile,
and some will look downcast.
In the case of the latter,
it shouldn't last.

Trials take place,
it's part of life,
but please remember,
you have the life of Christ.

For so many years,
you clearly rebelled,
but then God saved you,
from the fires of Hell.

He granted eternal life,
on streets of gold.
This alone,
should bring joy to your soul.

Jesus provided deliverance,
and set you free.
He says to take your problems,
and give them to Me.

Consider the Lord,
and what He has done.
There's no problem He can't handle,
not a single one.

So put a smile on your face,
and call on His name.
Trust in Him,
and to victory lay claim.

OCTOBER 15

CONFRONT YOUR PROBLEMS

Christians must confront their problems.
It's ultimately detrimental to hide from them.
Besides it's not God's way to overlook,
but it is God's way to confront.

Problems not dealt with will grow in time.
They'll become larger and more complex,
and may even appear hopeless,
if approached with neglect.

It's erroneous to respond in a sinful way,
in trying to overcome adverse situations.
Sin leads to sin,
and will result in further complications.

Doing a wrong to overcome a wrong,
will lead to guilt and depression.
Wrong feelings, behavior and habits must be examined,
when dealing with wrong situations.

Now look at these areas in light of God's Word.
Examine each area for sins of disobedience.
Biblical responses must be chosen,
after confession to God of sins and follow-on repentance.

Avoid band-aid solutions,
and don't play games with yourself.
The more honest you are,
the more you help yourself.

It may not be easy,
but you can ask God for help.
Trust He heard your heart's cry,
when in prayer you knelt.

Obedience is important,
for it's the way to do right.
It's essential to break bad habits,
while you keep the Word of God in sight.

OCTOBER 16

SILENT BAND MEMBERS

Look at the musicians.
With instruments in hand,
they're getting ready,
to strike up the band.

Look at the violinist.
She's playing her strings,
but I quickly notice,
I can't hear anything.

Look over there,
right at the drummer.
He's playing the drums,
but there's not even a mummer.

Look at the pianist.
He's playing his keys,
but there isn't any sound,
that has reached me.

There's something strange,
about this band.
There's no sound from the musicians,
neither woman or man.

I then began to ponder,
the meaning of this sight,
because I knew,
that something wasn't right.

They may have been musicians,
but nothing was heard.
I guess it's like that with Christians,
who never spread the Word.

They may be saved,
but they never share about Christ,
with unsaved others,
so they can receive new life.

OCTOBER 17

BE ENCOURAGED

Disappointment comes in life,
no one is immune,
but don't let it sit,
get over it soon.

Encourage yourself,
in the Lord,
and claim His promises,
using His Word.

Make melody in your heart,
and lift praises to the King.
You'll feel the affects,
as you begin to sing.

God inhabits the praises,
of His own,
as they ascend,
unto His throne.

His eye is on you,
He won't let you down.
He knows where you live,
in your hometown.

As you ponder His promises,
and consider them dear,
know for certain,
that He is near.

Trust in Him,
He sees your tears.
He's there to help you,
to chase your fears.

So be encouraged,
in the Lord,
and be confident,
in His Word.

Come out of that valley,
to higher ground,
for things are changing,
in the spirit realm.

You have a better report,
some inside information.
Your path is growing brighter,
you have the revelation.

OCTOBER 18

GET OUT OF THE DUGOUT

Life is played,
day after day,
year after year.
Listen to what I say.

Christians form this team.
There's a part for all.
Each has a part,
to play with the ball.

The field is set.
The game is on.
Don't stay in the dugout,
and sit there long.

Get into position,
no one is barred.
This is a team effort,
so play real hard.

Be all you can be,
and do what you can do,
to spread the gospel,
no matter who.

Help out at church,
and be sure to pray.
Be sure to give,
but I have more to say.

Pass out tracts,
and share on salvation.
Take the message,
to your part of the nation.

"Batter up."
Go to the plate.
Now get in the game,
it's not too late.

OCTOBER 19

CRESCENDO

The music is playing,
and it's not a lullaby.
The tempo is increasing,
as time goes by.

Volume is increasing,
it's easy to hear.
If you haven't noticed,
then please check your ears.

Instruments have been added,
and the scales are upbeat.
The music is building,
as you listen from seat.

A crescendo is coming,
and soon there'll be climax.
The crescendo that's coming,
is backed by biblical facts.

The end of the ages,
is upon this generation.
It's known as the last days,
and is said without hesitation.

The Lord will soon return,
this isn't a fictional story.
He'll be coming back,
in all of His glory.

The music is playing,
and you can't change its tune.
As you listen closely,
you know He's coming soon.

Sit up and take notice,
and listen with ears.
A crescendo is coming,
and it's coming real near.

OCTOBER 20

YOUR FACE HAS CHANGED

Take prayer out of schools,
and make it unconstitutional.
Ensure abortion is available,
and make it institutional.

Develop a society,
where no one's to blame,
for their criminal deeds,
and evil schemes.

Help them to know,
that they can sue,
and that they'll probably win,
when they do.

Use television and radio,
to pump pornography,
immorality and violence,
into the society.

Elect politicians,
who'll lie through their teeth,
to promote their own agendas,
and retain their seats.

Give people a free ride,
and let them know,
the government will care for them,
wherever they go.

Ensure all groups have rights,
and make it a free for all,
who cares about order,
and the good of all.

You'll notice in America,
that its face has changed.
It's an uglier picture,
that brings much shame.

A key reason exists,
for all of this mess.
Our Heavenly Father,
will surely attest.

It's a spiritual condition,
which is the source.
Turn from God,
and you change your course.

OCTOBER 21

HANDS AND FEET

Hands and feet,
are of great worth.
Just ask anybody,
on this earth.

They function in the body,
as important limbs,
performing many duties,
all of them.

The head sends directions,
and they execute,
receiving their signals,
and following suit.

The Head of the Church,
Jesus by name,
uses us,
in a similar vein.

Work gets done,
in natural ways,
with hands and feet,
throughout each day.

So it is with Christ,
and the great commission,
with the spreading of the gospel,
and our submission.

God's work is accomplished,
as Christians are used,
to share with the world,
and spread the good news.

Your hands and feet,
are important to Christ.
Trust in Him,
to work through your life.

OCTOBER 22

ARE YOU ASHAMED OF JESUS?

In the privacy of night,
Nicodemus did come,
to try and talk,
to God's dear Son.

A member of the Sanhedrin,
he didn't want to be seen,
by the other Pharisees,
in a daylight scene.

Think of his position,
and what they would think.
They might perceive,
there was a serious link.

It must be said,
that coming to Jesus was great,
but this story provides a point,
on which to meditate.

Many people come to Jesus,
and proceed to get saved,
but often you can't tell it,
by the way they behave.

Surrounded by men,
who don't believe,
they don't share their light,
so these men could receive.

Surrounded by men,
who curse at His name,
they remain silent,
and almost hide in shame.

Are these Christians afraid,
of what others would think?
If this is the case,
then their thinking stinks.

OCTOBER 23

HARVEST TIME

The farmer looks out,
after a morning rain,
as he surveys his wheat,
across the plain.

Experience tells him,
time is getting close,
for harvest time,
as he looks from fence post.

He senses the time,
and through sound reason,
starts to prepare,
for this harvest season.

He prepares his machines,
and lines up his men,
to work real hard,
for a good harvest end.

As you look around the world,
and check the signs,
you have to conclude,
we're in the end times.

It's time to prepare,
and roll up our sleeves,
and to get busy,
like honey bees.

Harvest windows close,
and then it's too late,
to gather the wheat,
so don't hesitate.

Join God's team,
and help harvest the wheat.
You have a part,
to make it more complete.

OCTOBER 24

OVERCOME EVIL WITH GOOD

Believers are to overcome evil with good.
They are not to be overcome by evil,
but are to overcome evil by returning good,
which sends a message of defeat to the devil.

Win battles God's way.
When persecuted, bless the accuser.
Don't react with cursing,
or you'll be like the persecutor.

The believer behaves this way,
out of his love for God.
To the world it may seem strange,
or even odd.

Love does not retaliate.
Fools do this and it spreads more evil.
This isn't God's way,
for you to deal with evil.

Respect what is good in the sight of all.
Seek peace with everyone including unbelievers.
Believers must act responsibly and not provoke
more trouble,
for this is the way of true believers.

Revenge is not to be sought,
against antagonizing unbelievers.
God says it's His job,
and not the job of the believer.

Heap coals upon their heads,
is what the Bible does say.
That applies to all believers,
even when the flesh would sway.

Walking in love,
is not always easy to do,
but if you're a believer,
it applies to you.

OCTOBER 25

LIFE'S GOAL

Life goes on,
day after day,
If this sounds mundane,
then listen to what I say.

Many in the church,
go day after day,
not thinking of souls,
nor getting them saved.

The heart of God,
centers around salvation of souls.
To the born again Christian,
this should never get old.

God is ready,
to touch each life,
if we'll do our work,
and share of Christ.

Remember the words,
concerning the feast,
when pursuit was made,
to even gather the least.

Compel them to come in,
were words that were heard.
It's time for all of us,
to give heed to those words.

Christ was clear,
when He gave the great commission.
He said to spread the Word,
if we will listen.

You have the green light,
so get busy with souls.
Stir your heart,
and make it a life's goal.

OCTOBER 26

24 HOURS

People are born with different abilities,
and many different traits.
Some will accomplish little,
and some will accomplish great.

People develop different trades,
and develop different careers.
Some people you'll like,
and some you won't endear.

There are differences in people,
it's really crystal clear,
but there's a common link,
that all people share.

No matter who you are,
there's a common thread,
that applies to all folks,
who aren't yet dead.

Time is that link,
of which I allude.
Everyone has 24 hours in a day,
with no one to exclude.

This was granted by God,
it was by specific design,
that all should have equal day,
of what is called time.

What people do within it,
affects so many things,
not only in this world,
but also in the unseen.

So use your time wisely,
a wise steward be.
Use it wisely,
and not wastefully.

OCTOBER 27

IS HE SPECIAL TO YOU?

Is Jesus special to you?
Do you ever take time,
just to say things,
like I love you?

Do you ever take time,
to offer thankfulness,
in appreciation,
for His faithfulness?

Do you ever take time,
to offer praise,
even for a moment,
during your day?

Do you ever take time,
to offer worship,
in appreciation,
for your relationship?

It's so easy to say,
Jesus, I love you.
If you don't do this,
then I encourage you to do.

Ten lepers were healed,
but only one came back.
Will you be as the one,
or stay with the pack?

Is Jesus special to you?
He died for your sins,
and into His kingdom,
brought you in.

Make yourself appreciative,
towards your precious Lord.
You should often say,
I love you, Lord.

OCTOBER 28

STAY WITH CHRIST

Lot and his wife,
were told to make haste,
from Sodom and Gomorrah,
towns of disgrace.

Keep on going,
and do not look back,
were the directions of God,
that were clear without lack.

For they did know,
from God's instruction,
that Sodom and Gomorrah,
were to reap destruction.

Hurried they went,
from this den of iniquity,
areas well known,
for their deeds of infamy.

A pillar of salt,
Lot's wife became,
for she looked back,
only herself to blame.

The life of the Christian,
must remain steadfast,
and leave the world's filth,
in their past.

Don't give up Christ,
and return to the world.
These words apply,
to both boy or girl.

I will advise you,
that to take this course,
will only bring sadness,
with great remorse.

Perhaps these words,
have an alarming sound,
but receive this truth,
or be on dangerous ground.

Now I'll close,
but please be sure,
to stay with Jesus,
and resist the world's lures.

OCTOBER 29

GREATEST MISCALCULATION

I want to take some time,
and address the greatest miscalculation,
in the life of man.
I say this without hesitation.

There have been many miscalculations,
throughout the history of time.
Battles of war are filled with them,
as revealed through devastating after signs.

War isn't the only place,
where there have been miscalculations.
It's common in the lives of people,
who haven't made wise preparations.

It's common in business,
where people did not correctly foresee,
the trends of markets,
and the way they would be.

You can easily see,
that miscalculations create quite a list,
but there's clearly one greater,
than all of this.

He was a majestic angel,
Lucifer by name.
He rebelled against God,
and was cast out in shame.

This gross miscalculation,
is still seen today.
Man thinks he can rebel,
and do it his own way.

To refuse Jesus as Lord,
and rebel against God's plan,
is to make the greatest miscalculation,
known to man.

OCTOBER 30

DEALING WITH PEOPLE

We all deal with people.
Sometimes people are nice,
and then sometimes,
people are not so nice.

A few thoughts on this subject,
might be of benefit.
So let's discuss some thoughts,
and in a few minutes fit.

Always be considerate,
and make it a rule.
Follow and practice it,
like you were still in school.

Never seek revenge,
but give it to the Lord.
It says to cast your cares on Him,
in His written Word.

Control your anger,
and use soft answers in reply,
even when your demeanor,
wants to belie.

Be obedient to God's direction,
first and foremost before man.
You please Him first,
as you make your stand.

Many will compromise their values,
to gain the approval of man.
When this violates your conscious,
you know you've compromised your stand.

When you deal with people,
try to keep these things in mind.
If you can apply these things,
they'll know you're of a special kind.

OCTOBER 31

FINGERPRINTS

Fingerprints are different,
for all mankind.
Each has his own,
with different lines.

Check people out closely,
and then you'll see,
that this is true,
whether it's he or she.

As fingerprints are different,
so is each human.
They all are different,
whether man or woman.

Each has different traits,
which cannot be denied.
It's like that with gifts,
that are found deep inside.

To know and glorify God,
man is called to do.
This applies to all,
no matter who.

Man should use his gifts,
towards God's glory,
for this honors God,
in each life's story.

Man should develop his gifts,
and use his skills,
in fulfilling God's plan,
as he lives.

For each one's life,
God does have a plan,
and it's a good one,
for both woman or man.

NOVEMBER 1

THE THREAT

A general prepares,
against the known threat,
preparing plans,
and getting them set.

A coach prepares,
and studies the offense,
wanting to devise,
a strong defense.

Fearful is the devil,
when a Christian learns.
It gets his attention,
and becomes a concern.

A Christian becomes,
a threat indeed,
when in his heart,
he plants good seed.

Know that your enemy,
is scared of you,
when you know the Word,
and of it do.

An effective Christian,
grounded in God,
gets the devil's attention,
with the quickest of nods.

The devil knows,
this is not a good sign,
so he devises plans,
with counter design.

"Set some traps,
along his way.
Create some things,
to ruin his day."

"Stop the growth,
and spread some doom,
for as he grows,
it brings us gloom."

Victory is ours,
if we remain diligent,
to stand on the Word,
and against traps be vigilant.

NOVEMBER 2

BIG BROTHER AND THE BULLY

Think about your youth,
and your days on the playground.
These kind of discussions apply,
to most any town.

Think about school,
and during times of recess.
Remember the bully,
that tried to cause a mess.

Many times a youth,
if he is overmatched,
would get a big brother,
with quick dispatch.

Now think about sin,
and the affects of evil.
Think about man's condition,
and his link with the devil.

Man fell in the garden,
many years ago.
This brought death and destruction,
with total bondage to show.

God so ordained,
that He would send a big brother,
to confront the bully,
and of sin to smother.

The bout was set,
during a short life span,
when Jesus defeated the devil,
and redeemed man.

He's the big brother,
to all Christians.
He'll be big brother to all others,
if to the gospel they'll listen.

NOVEMBER 3

GREAT COORDINATOR

Let's talk coordination.
Certain actions are required,
to effect positive results,
and accomplish what's desired.

Business goals and objectives,
are commonly set,
but it takes great effort and coordination,
to ensure they are met.

Knowledge, skills and desire,
are key attributes,
of a coordinator,
and one that contributes.

Let's now consider God,
and take some time,
to ponder these things,
within our minds.

Knowledge is no problem,
He's the Great Creator.
He knows how to get things done,
for He's a great facilitator.

Skills is no problem,
His abilities abound.
Believe in His talents,
and you'll be on solid ground.

Desire is no problem,
and to this lay clutch,
He only wants good for you,
because He loves you so much.

He has angelic hosts,
that He releases in lives,
to help coordinate details,
and bring good into lives.

When you pray to God,
trust in His might,
and all of His ability,
though you do not see by sight.

Be assured, He's there.
He's coordinating details,
and remember this,
He never fails.

NOVEMBER 4

FELLOWSHIP

Peer pressure affects.
It affects negatively,
and reciprocally,
it affects positively.

The company one keeps,
should be considered carefully.
This is very important,
and should not be taken lightly.

The Bible clearly states,
that bad company corrupts good morals.
As many people will attest,
this causes great sorrow.

So it is,
when considered in reverse,
when people keep company,
with those redeemed from the curse.

Good Christian fellowship,
will serve one well.
One should pursue this,
and with good Christians dwell.

This environment is conducive,
to times of edification.
It will also provide,
moments of exhortation.

Good Christian fellowship,
will reinforce,
biblical principles and values,
as people follow this course.

Gather in fellowship.
It's good to pursue.
Benefits will be gained,
if this you'll do.

NOVEMBER 5

SERVITUDE

Humility says much,
much more than pride.
It's the better of the two,
please take this in stride.

Humility of mind,
is desirable indeed.
It reaches out to others,
and promotes good deeds.

Be not selfish,
or have vain conceit,
acting arrogant,
is not real neat.

Look out for others,
and their interests as well.
They'll begin to take notice,
and think you're swell.

Serving others,
and being kind,
is not wasted effort,
but a good sign.

Jesus said,
to walk in love,
an important message,
from above.

You'll gain much,
from a walk like this,
and if you don't,
there'll be things you'll miss.

Your approach to life,
will show your attitude,
as actions reveal,
your degree of servitude.

NOVEMBER 6

KINDNESS AND TENDERNESS

So you're now a Christian.
It's certainly good news.
You made the winning decision,
where you just can't lose.

Rough edges are there,
but they'll be smoothed in time.
This brings something else up,
traits that are tender and kind.

Your spirit is reborn,
beneath your body facade.
Now living within you,
is the Spirit of God.

Within your spirit,
you'll find kindness,
and next to it,
you'll find tenderness.

The traits are there,
I'll guarantee,
but you must release them,
and set them free.

It's like a butterfly,
contained in a jar.
If you keep the lid shut,
he won't go far.

Lift the lid,
and he's now free,
released to the world,
it's easy to see.

Lift the lid,
and let them go,
out to others,
as God's love you show.

NOVEMBER 7

LOOK BEYOND

Elisha said to God,
"Open his eyes."
The servant's eyes were opened,
and there was a sigh.

Angels abounded,
creating an impending sight.
They were there for them,
if there was a fight.

Confidence quickly came,
to the servant's heart.
He knew they were protected,
for God would do His part.

Look beyond,
and open your eyes.
There's a spiritual realm,
you cannot deny.

God is real,
and so is His plan,
that of redemption,
available for each man.

God is real,
look beyond.
Let this sink in,
and to your heart dawn.

Live your life,
with that of focus.
No magic here,
no hocus-pocus.

Focus on God,
beginning now.
Look to the Bible,
it tells you how.

Live for Him now,
and if you do,
He'll help you along,
and provide good for you.

Then when you leave,
this earth's path,
you'll see great rewards,
that will forever last.

NOVEMBER 8

UNNECESSARY CASUALTIES

The platoon was ambushed.
It was not aware of the trap.
Their presence was followed,
it was like reading a map.

The pilot flew low,
too close to the ground.
As a result,
the plane was shot down.

While on patrol,
the boat hit a mine.
Crew observation was lax,
which was not a good sign.

Events such as these,
could have been changed.
Mistakes were made,
that brought casualties of shame.

Know your enemy,
and know your Bible.
Claim the promises,
to ensure your survival.

Knowledge is important,
as well as diligence.
During all phases of war,
there must be vigilance.

You're in a war,
I hope you know.
Spiritual warfare goes on,
no matter where you go.

It's a day-to-day walk,
a hardened fact,
so maintain your guard,
and never be lax.

NOVEMBER 9

SPIRIT OF EXCELLENCE

Develop good work habits.
Don't make them sloppy,
or your work will show,
that it is shoddy.

Your work will show,
as you slip a little here.
It will show,
as you slip a little there.

A spirit of excellence,
should be your mark.
Approach all tasks,
with this at start.

Be conscientious,
and know for sure,
as you do good work,
it will endure.

Be on time,
and don't be late.
It's speaks well,
no need to contemplate.

Work real hard,
and people will know,
that you do good work,
for it will show.

Be not lazy,
but diligent with hands.
Over the course of time,
it'll be appreciated by men.

A spirit of excellence,
pursue with zest.
Over a period of time,
people will know you're the best.

NOVEMBER 10

GRASS IS GREENER

The grass is greener,
is a story of old.
In the Book of Genesis,
it was clearly told.

Adam and Eve,
well known by name,
thought the grass was greener,
which brought them shame.

The grass is greener,
is still common today.
It's still used by Satan,
to get people to sway.

Catch that girl,
in the tight sweater.
Life with her,
would truly be better.

That's right.
Leave your wife.
She's now boring,
and doesn't entice.

Split the church,
and go your way.
Many will follow,
if you try to sway.

The grass is greener.
It's the same old tune,
but many find out,
it's not a boon.

Follow the Word,
and don't fall prey,
for the grass may have fleas,
listen to what I say.

NOVEMBER 11

SUPPLY DEPARTMENT

Military personnel,
get issued equipment,
and various clothing items,
from the Supply department.

The Supply department issues,
and people receive.
It's like that with the heart,
and what you believe.

The issues of life,
come out of the heart.
It's what you believe,
that sets your mark.

The Supply department issues,
what it has to give.
Your heart issues,
on how you're going to live.

What's in your heart,
will come out.
It'll affect your life,
have no doubt.

Stock your heart's shelves,
with materials of good.
Build up your faith,
is how you should.

Take the Word of God,
and pack it in.
You'll need it there,
to be strong within.

What you stock,
will directly affect,
your issues of life,
so do not neglect.

NOVEMBER 12

LICENSE TO OPERATE

A license is required,
to operate your car.
You need it to drive,
whether near or far.

To operate your business,
a license is required.
You must have it,
even if not desired.

To go hunting,
or even fish,
a license is required,
the law does list.

To operate on earth's soil,
the same is true.
A license is required,
to do what you do.

You have a license,
if you breathe.
It was at birth,
that you received.

Into a body,
your spirit did enter.
You now may operate,
during spring, summer, fall and winter.

An on fire Christian,
in his license to operate,
makes the devil tremble,
and even shake.

He affects Satan's kingdom,
as his prayers ring strong.
He seeks man's good,
as he opposes wrong.

I imagine,
the devil loves,
to see Christians leave their bodies,
and go above.

While in their bodies,
they propose a threat.
So he'll try to revoke their licenses,
if they'll let.

NOVEMBER 13

PRAYER CLOSET

A prayer closet,
how is it defined?
Is it configured,
in some kind of design?

Is it a closet,
that has a floor,
where people kneel,
behind the door?

I will now attempt,
to better define,
the term prayer closet,
in a more biblical line.

It's in your spirit,
where you get alone with God.
You determine the location,
wherever on the earth's sod.

Concerning the world's affairs,
you shut the door.
You may even pray standing or walking,
not necessarily on the floor.

This time is between you and God.
You commune with Him.
He's concerned about all your prayers,
each and every one of them.

Prayer is vital to the spirit.
It's like air in your lungs.
It's an important part of your walk,
and must not be left unsung.

No situation with God,
should be considered too bleak.
Always remember in Christ,
you've been made complete.

Never give up,
when you come to the Lord.
Remain consistent in prayer,
and He'll honor His Word.

Times spent in your prayer closet,
can be life giving.
Times spent in your prayer closet,
can be Hell shaking.

NOVEMBER 14

COME BACK TO THE MIRROR

You stand in front of the mirror,
and look at your face.
You then quickly turn,
and depart with haste.

Appointments to keep,
and places to go,
but there's something to consider,
something to know.

You know how you look,
most people do,
but the Bible talks about this,
if you want a clue.

People hear the Word,
but then don't do it.
It's compared to your face in the mirror,
but you don't remember it.

Hearing the Word alone,
doesn't bring total victory.
Being a doer of what you heard,
is exceptionally key.

The next time you hear the Word,
make sure you do it.
This is of great importance,
so please do not omit.

Hide the Word in your spirit.
Meditate on its content.
Now put it into practice,
and be a doer of it.

If you hear only,
and do not implement,
then please come back to the mirror,
and look for a moment.

NOVEMBER 15

TIME LAPSE PHOTOGRAPHY

Time lapse photography,
is interesting to see.
Picture the budding flower,
or a leaf on a tree.

The bud or leaf develops,
right before your very eyes.
Pretty soon you'll observe,
it's grown to full size.

In just a few seconds,
time has been condensed.
Changes took place over time,
the photography shows evidence.

Day by day,
negligible growth was seen.
So in reference to the Christian,
what does this mean?

Sometimes a Christian,
will begin to ponder,
if he's developing in growth,
and will begin to wonder.

Sometimes it seems,
that he's stuck in place.
It's at these times,
that I remind you of God's grace.

Things are happening,
as you do what you can do.
Always remember,
He's working on you.

Your flower is developing.
It's captured on God's film.
Just remain in the Word,
and trust in Him.

NOVEMBER 16

SILENCE

Hustling through the woods,
one misses much.
I learned this as a youth,
when reality touched.

On one autumn day,
I proceeded to the woods.
I sat down on the leaves,
and became as quiet as I could.

It was interesting to hear,
some different sounds,
that I previously hadn't heard,
when I sat on the ground.

Squirrels came out,
and were interesting to see,
as they went along merrily,
right before me.

Sights and sounds,
became so clear,
as if to the animals,
I wasn't near.

This is a lesson for prayer.
We must slow down,
from our daily activities,
and leave the bustling sounds.

Become quiet before God,
and listen from your spirit.
Leave the noise and cares of the day,
and just do it.

Spend quiet time with Him.
It's a quality decision.
You can be assured,
you have His permission.

NOVEMBER 17

NO DEPOSIT, NO RETURN

To open a bank account,
money is required.
As deposits are made,
growth will transpire.

With each deposit,
the account will grow.
As you check each statement,
you'll see it shows.

If there's no investment,
then there will be no return.
This is quite simple,
and easy to learn.

Check your spirit,
can you find the Word?
It'll be there,
if good Word you've heard.

Investment in heart,
requires your time.
Investment in heart,
requires your dime.

Attend a good church,
and get taught well.
Listen intently,
and on the Word do dwell.

Listen to good tapes,
and read good books.
You're making deposits,
no matter how it looks.

The Word will profit,
there'll be return,
but investment is required,
as we've just learned.

Make time for the Word,
and build your account.
Make deposits in your heart,
with increasing amounts.

Return will show,
at the needed times.
Return will show,
with good signs.

NOVEMBER 18

BEST CLOTHING

People buy clothes,
for changes of climate.
Temperature changes,
provide first hints.

People buy clothes,
to stay in style.
On this comment,
there'll be no denial.

People buy clothes,
just on whim.
It's simply because,
they like them.

Clothing protects,
and clothing speaks,
and on this point,
your attention I seek.

No matter what you wear,
there's something better.
You can read all about it,
in the New Testament letters.

It certainly protects,
and speaks real strong.
By making this choice,
you can never go wrong.

It's the Blood of Jesus.
Receive Jesus first,
into your heart,
and receive the new birth.

Then plead His Blood,
and draw its line,
around you and your family,
during daily time.

The devil knows,
what this means.
It affects his operations,
and foils his schemes.

Cloth yourself in the Blood.
It's the best clothing you can obtain.
Avail yourself to its benefits,
and to it lay claim.

NOVEMBER 19

BOOT CAMP

Young civilians arrive on buses,
and report to the base.
The drill instructor meets them,
and gets them moving with haste.

Attitude adjustments,
begin to be made,
as the soldiers react,
to the drill instructor's aid.

In the coming days,
lessons will be learned.
There's a spiritual analogy,
that can be discerned.

To become an effective soldier,
instruction is required,
to help the soldier improve,
even when his flesh does not desire.

To become an effective Christian,
instruction is required,
to help the Christian improve,
even when his flesh does not desire.

Traits are molded into the soldier.
A behavior that's disciplined,
starts to evolve,
from that of being undisciplined.

A trait of dedication,
begins to show.
More knowledge is sought,
with the desire to know.

It becomes remarkably clear,
as the soldiers march in formation,
that changes have occurred,
resulting in this transformation.

Poor habits of young Christians,
must also be replaced,
if they are to grow,
under God's grace.

Boot camp is important,
for soldier or Christian.
Let the soldier of Christ,
give ear and listen.

NOVEMBER 20

REWARDER

The term reward,
is easy to perceive,
for if you do something,
then you're going to receive.

Now take a moment,
and consider what you heard,
where it says to gather,
in the Lord's Word.

It takes energy and effort,
to pay attention,
during the church service,
but there's more to mention.

Studying the Bible,
line upon line,
chapter upon chapter,
certainly takes time.

Time spent in reading good books,
certainly demands personal cost,
but this along with listening to good tapes,
should not be considered time lost.

Now consider this,
if you dare,
of all your petitions,
and hours of prayer.

Continue to trust God,
for your time and effort has been noted.
Continuc to trust God,
for your time and effort has not been wasted.

God is a rewarder,
of those that diligently seek Him.
Rewards are coming to many Christians,
so continue to look for them.

NOVEMBER 21

PYRITE

When one spots pyrite,
one is apt to believe,
that it's of great value,
but they're deceived.

Upon spotting pyrite,
people may exclaim,
and get all excited,
as they lay claim.

The glitter attracts them,
and draws them near.
Thinking it's of great value,
they hold it dear.

Pyrite has another name,
it's known as fool's gold.
It doesn't have great value,
perhaps you've been told.

Thus it is with man,
and the choices he makes.
If he chooses to live for the world,
he makes a great mistake.

If he chooses pyrite,
instead of real gold,
he'll find he'll lose,
his very soul.

He may laugh,
and sing real loud,
while he lives for the world,
and pleases the crowd.

Then he will die,
and realize it wasn't gold,
but pyrite,
that claimed his soul.

The fool's gold of life,
has fooled many.
Thinking it was of great value,
it was only worth pennies.

Don't choose pyrite,
but choose real gold.
Accept the Lord Jesus,
and save your soul.

NOVEMBER 22

NOTICE THE IMAGE

The artist uses his brush,
and begins to paint.
A little here and a little there,
it's like that with the saint.

Colors are mixed,
and different brush strokes used,
to develop the painting,
with various hues.

The artist realizes,
that time is required,
to do a quality work,
which is his desire.

The canvas begins to reveal,
a beautiful scene.
Although it's not finished,
there's something to be gleaned.

As the artist works,
and continues to paint,
realize that's how God works,
on his saints.

Little by little,
God works away,
on his saints,
throughout their days.

Notice the image,
that's starting to shape.
You'll begin to see Jesus,
and some of His traits.

As the painting evolves,
you'll see what I mean.
Qualities of good are blended,
to develop this beautiful scene.

NOVEMBER 23

THE VENUS'S-FLYTRAP

The Venus's-flytrap,
provides an interesting sight,
when a fly lands on it,
from its flight.

Watch the fly,
pick out a limb.
Each provides a trap,
every one of them.

The fly does not know,
what's in store for him,
when he decides to land,
on one of those limbs.

Once he lands,
the grip is made,
as the plant moves swiftly,
without delay.

Struggle as he will,
he's now caught,
as in a vice grip,
with troubles fraught.

The devil has set traps.
To some drugs appeal,
but for many that land,
drugs will kill.

Some turn to alcohol,
or into pornography slip.
In either case,
there's a strong grip.

Make no mistake.
No matter the vice,
it has been designed with hurt,
to take your spiritual life.

Amid the travail,
some may die physically,
but the schemes ultimately are designed,
to take lives spiritually.

Don't fly into the traps.
Land in a better place,
by accepting the Lord Jesus,
and His gift of grace.

NOVEMBER 24

SHOOT THE GUERRILLA

He slyly moves in,
with clandestine skill,
and whispers into the man's ears,
words that appeal.

He came with purpose,
to disturb this man's life,
to rob him of peace,
and get him in strife.

With the stealth of a guerrilla,
he now moves away,
and begins to watch with glee,
the ensuing fray.

The man does not see,
with his spiritual eyes.
Those thoughts were not his,
but he doesn't realize.

He blames himself,
and rightly so,
but there's so much more,
that he should know.

He needs to realize,
that the devil is real,
and has come against him,
with desire to steal.

He needs to load his gun,
when the devil comes around,
with the Word of God,
and send him out of town.

He needs to shoot the guerrilla,
and speak the Word,
with the gun of his mouth,
and the devil will run away scared.

NOVEMBER 25

DON'T PLAY WITH EXPLOSIVES

Blasting caps are sensitive,
and can easily go off.
Better treat them gently,
and at this not scoff.

The handling of explosives,
such as dynamite,
must be handled carefully,
or it could be your last night.

It doesn't take much,
to cause a detonation.
I state this clearly,
without slightest hesitation.

Play with explosives,
and prepare to get burned.
Ignore sound advice,
and a hard way you'll learn.

Jump into sin.
After all, you can always quit,
but it's not always so,
if you want a hint.

It happens to others,
but never to you.
Many people think this way,
sure they do.

What's that in your hand?
Is it a blasting cap?
Don't play with it,
or there'll be a mishap.

Tears can be saved,
if you'll heed my advice.
Don't play with sin,
and save your life.

Don't jump into sin,
and go down the wrong path.
Its pleasures deceive,
and will not last.

Turn to Christ,
and you'll be on solid ground.
You'll quickly find,
there'll be new joy found.

NOVEMBER 26

HE WATCHES AND LISTENS

There's someone watching,
wherever you go.
Every act you do,
He does know.

There's someone listening,
wherever you go.
Every word you speak,
He does know.

Sit on the couch,
and watch television.
Be assured,
you're within His vision.

Conversations at work,
He stands real near.
You can be assured,
you have His ear.

Take a trip,
to a distant location.
He's also there,
on your vacation.

Go to the ocean,
and visit the beach.
Whatever you say,
is within His reach.

Get in disagreements,
He's right there,
for He's interested,
in all your affairs.

Jesus watches and listens,
as you come and leave.
Throughout the day,
do your actions please?

NOVEMBER 27

GET RID OF EGYPTIAN THINKING

The Israelites left Egypt,
with triumphant sounds.
They left to take possession,
of promised ground.

At the Red Sea they came,
chased by Pharaoh's men,
where the Israelites crossed,
but not the Egyptians.

The waters parted,
but then the waters fell back,
to swallow up the Egyptians,
a well known fact.

God delivered the Israelites,
and told them to go forth,
to take possession of the promised land,
and proceed on course.

The Israelites began to doubt,
after spying out the land.
It made many of their men,
to begin to cower within.

After beginning to doubt,
fear had set in,
as many began to ponder,
about Egypt within.

Many began to speak out loud,
about returning to Egypt,
and all of its bondage,
from the words of their lips.

Doubt and fear,
brought on Egyptian thinking.
In the nostrils of God,
this was certainly stinking.

It might be said,
if you want a good tip,
that it took the Israelites 40 years,
to make an 11 day trip.

For results in God,
you must trust in His Word.
Don't think in the way,
of the story you just heard.

NOVEMBER 28

REBELLION

Rebellion is not new.
It started with Adam and Eve,
back in the garden,
when Eve was deceived.

Rebellion occurred against Moses.
Korah opposed his authority,
and as a result,
gained biblical notoriety.

As time has past,
rebellion is still seen.
Check any location,
or most any scene.

People reject the law,
with defiant looks.
It's easy to see,
the rebellious hooks.

Rebellion against parents,
today is quite evident.
If you look around,
you'll see it's prevalent.

Check prison cells,
and you will find,
rebellious people,
now serving time.

The cemetery reveals,
its destructive path,
where people lie,
in graves with grass.

A rebellious path,
has dangerous curves.
So steer away,
and to it not serve.

NOVEMBER 29

NEVER GIVE UP

At your lowest moment,
never give up.
No matter the situation,
never give up.

When the outlook looks bleak,
never give up.
When your morale is low,
never give up.

When others are against you,
never give up.
When the odds are against you,
never give up.

When things come against you,
never give up.
When disappointments show,
never give up.

When you're tired,
never give up.
When you've been falsely accused,
never give up.

When man can't help,
never give up.
When you need a miracle,
never give up.

Lift up your eyes,
no need to get down.
There's nothing too hard,
that God can't turn around.

Never give up.
Come to the Lord Jesus.
God can handle all your problems,
each and every one of them.

NOVEMBER 30

THE ENEMY'S WAR ROOM

Let's take a visit,
to observe Satan's strategy,
presented to his demons,
to effect great tragedy.

The room is filled,
as Satan briefs his plan,
to his demon commanders,
his strategy against man.

His strategy has three major points.
First, inflate the ego.
Pump it up with pride,
wherever man goes.

Secondly, satisfy the flesh.
To man's flesh appeal.
Apply this well,
and souls you'll steal.

Thirdly, love the world.
Get man to love the world.
Start on them early,
when they're boys and girls.

Tested against time,
Satan's strategy remains the same.
His orders are consistent,
they haven't changed.

Multitudes have fallen,
and have been taken as prey,
but it need not happen to you,
if you'll listen to what I say.

Receive the Blood of Jesus,
and have your old nature purged.
Begin to grow in Him,
and you'll triumphantly emerge.

Jesus whipped the devil.
Let this mystery not confound.
He did it for you,
to set you on victory's ground.

A victim of Satan,
not in your case,
if you come to the Lord Jesus,
and receive His grace.

DECEMBER 1

LOOKING FOR A PLACE

Let's take a drive,
through the streets.
Please get in,
and take a seat.

Keep your eyes open,
and check the street signs.
They'll remind you of people,
and its different kinds.

There's Sin Alley,
to the right of your seat.
It's next to Sickness Lane,
and Barely Get Along Street.

Let's move ahead,
to Doubt and Fear Row.
Let's not stop here,
there are more streets to go.

We'll now turn this way,
and go towards Salvation Lane.
The houses are looking better,
I do proclaim.

This area looks better,
I must report.
Look over there,
it's Faith Court.

Healthy Street,
is just up ahead,
next to Prosperity Drive,
just like I said.

Looking for a place,
you might want to live?
I've got some recommendations,
that I can give.

I know a great realtor,
who will treat you right.
He gave His all,
so you could get a top site.

Meet the Lord Jesus.
He knows all the streets.
You can make a deal with Him,
that just can't be beat.

DECEMBER 2

NO TICKET REQUIRED

A car is one way,
to go from Gary, Indiana,
crossing a few states,
to get to Phoenix, Arizona.

One probably would use a plane,
to go from America,
crossing the Pacific Ocean,
to get to South Korea.

A train might be used,
if you're in Germany,
to go through some mountains,
to get to Italy.

A cruise is one means,
to go from Florida,
throughout the Caribbean Islands,
to get to Panama.

Buses are commonly seen,
as an alternative to the car,
carrying people,
both near and far.

People are separated by distances,
and need transportation,
if they're going to arrive,
at their desired locations.

In the physical realm,
there is no space elimination.
Man must travel distances,
to get to his desired location.

In the spiritual realm,
there is no distance in prayer.
Your presence can be felt,
without you being there.

No matter where you live,
I say without hesitation,
that you can pray for anyone,
and reach them in their nation.

No ticket is required,
to board this plane,
just a willing and loving heart,
that seeks change.

DECEMBER 3

GREEN APPLES

Don't eat green apples,
before their time.
Just the color green,
should provide a warning sign.

A sour taste,
you will receive,
because of the unripeness,
you did not perceive.

Ripeness will come,
in due time,
as green turns to red,
providing a good sign.

As it is with apples,
so it is with man,
as God develops him,
and works His plan.

I say this emphatically,
that God has a plan,
determined before birth,
for each woman and man.

Years in the desert,
on Moses were spent,
developing him for an assignment,
when to Pharaoh he was sent.

Things must be developed,
through experience and time.
Stay with God's timetable,
and things will be fine.

Be diligent and patient,
and trust in God's hand.
In your life He's working,
to develop His plan.

DECEMBER 4

POLLY WANTS A CRACKER

"Polly wants a cracker,"
so the parrot speaks.
People hear these words,
and think they're neat.

For the bird to mimic,
is considered quite a feat,
but that's all it is,
when the parrot speaks.

A Christian that speaks,
and proclaims in God's Name,
should not be like the parrot,
and do only the same.

He should have the promise,
down in his spirit.
So when he speaks,
it's more than mimic.

One way to help,
is to meditate,
on the promise of God,
in a pensive state.

Begin to imagine,
the result you desire.
Let it set,
in your heart a fire.

Coupled with this,
continue to speak.
Keep on doing this,
if results you seek.

Soon you'll find,
the words you proclaim,
are rising from your heart,
with results to claim.

Speaking is important,
most assuredly yes,
but you must believe,
to get God's best.

Believe and speak,
provide the right combination.
Use them together,
to obtain your manifestation.

DECEMBER 5

GOD WANTS TO USE YOU

Come with me,
and let's conduct a review,
of some of God's mighty servants.
It'll be good for you.

First, consider Moses.
A murderer was he,
before he went into exile,
and from Egypt did flee.

Now look at David.
He too was a murderer,
but in addition to that,
he was also an adulterer.

Consider Mary Magdalene.
A harlot was she,
before she met Jesus,
and was set free.

Take the prophet Elijah.
After his great victory over Baal,
he fled in great fear,
at the threats of Jezebel.

Don't forget Peter.
He later became a strong man,
but only after denying the Lord three times,
and not taking a stand.

Noah was a man of faith,
but he also got drunk.
This is recorded in the Bible,
and is not bunk.

Jonah ran from God.
His attitude was poor.
God had to deal with him,
to get him to open his heart's door.

Get the picture.
Mighty men of God made mistakes.
No matter where you are,
it's not too late.

God wants to use you.
Turn to Him.
He'll forgive your past,
no matter what sin.

DECEMBER 6

LIFE IS A MIST

While at Niagara Falls,
I could easily see,
a rising mist,
set before me.

The water would tumble,
over the edge,
while I safely observed,
from a fenced in ledge.

The water would hit,
on the surface below,
bringing to remembrance,
something I already know.

A mist would be created,
from the sudden force,
that began to ascend,
from its liquid source.

Upwards it goes,
for a short period of time,
and then it disappears,
leaving no sign.

A life is born,
to commence its days,
to live on the earth,
come what may.

It may live long,
with years numbering ninety,
or it may pass early,
with years numbering twenty.

In either case,
life is short,
when compared to eternity,
or recorded time's report.

Life is here,
and then it's gone,
much like a mist,
or a short song.

So live for Christ,
and this I'll say,
make your time count,
throughout all your day.

DECEMBER 7

SOMETHING YOU WANT TO DO

This message is for the world.
To one who has an ear,
listen to my words,
and please do hear.

I want to discuss an exercise program.
It concerns knee bends.
If you have an exercise program,
then include them in.

I recommend to start doing knee bends,
for those that don't exercise.
It would not only help your knees,
but also your thighs.

Exercising your knees,
will give you flexibility,
for there's coming a time,
when it will be a necessity.

There's an inevitable appointment in time,
when all will be required,
to bow their knees,
for it has been decreed.

Every knee will bow,
and every tongue will confess,
that Jesus is Lord,
no need to contest.

People can do it now,
or they can do it later,
but doing it now,
is so much better.

While you have breath,
you can receive salvation.
Receive His love now,
to avoid eternal damnation.

His love is wonderful.
He'll be your best friend,
He died on the cross,
to redeem you from all sins.

When you come to the Lord Jesus,
it'll be easy to bow your knee.
It's something you want to do,
just wait and see.

DECEMBER 8

WAGON TRAIN

In American history,
there came a time,
when people went west,
with dreams sublime.

Load the wagons,
and hitch the horses,
as they moved,
on different courses.

Some went towards Oregon,
and some towards Santa Fe.
No matter the route,
it made for long days.

Troubles occurred,
along these dusty routes,
but they had to move on,
to accomplish their pursuits.

Rain would come,
and in some cases snow.
Mountains would come,
but over they would go.

They realized among them,
that no matter the weather,
they had to keep going,
and work together.

Sickness would come,
but onward they would go.
They had to be tough,
and persistence show.

Difficulties occurred,
but many arrived,
at their destinations,
and survived.

Life still has difficulties.
Most people will agree,
but there's something here,
that we can receive.

You have to keep on,
to fulfill your dreams.
Be strong in the Blood of Jesus,
and overcome the devil's schemes.

DECEMBER 9

YOU'RE IN COVENANT

With sling in hand,
and speed afoot,
David moved quickly,
with steadfast look.

His eyes were fixed,
as he crossed the battle line.
There were no signs of weakness,
of any kind.

Goliath taunted,
and cursed Jesse's son,
but little did he know,
the strength in David's run.

David had a covenant,
with the Most High God.
To this oppressive giant,
He would not cower or dodge.

He trusted God,
and refused to be shamed,
by one out of covenant,
cursing God's Holy Name.

Within his heart,
he knew victory was ahead,
as he told Goliath,
he was about to sever his head.

With bold assurance,
and words that proclaimed,
David trusted his God,
and to victory laid claim.

Run to your battle line,
with no sign of fear,
for you're in covenant,
with a God who's near.

DECEMBER 10

FAITH HAS REST

Anxiety is not found in faith.
Worry also is not found.
This applies to anywhere you go,
whether city or town.

God is real,
but you're not Him.
When you give your problems to God,
He then has them.

You're now trusting in Him.
There's no need to fret,
Time to rest in peace,
and not get upset.

Always remember this,
that faith has rest.
If you're in faith,
it'll pass this test.

God's working on your behalf.
So do what you can do,
but please do remember,
He's the one working it out for you.

As you remain in peace,
fear and doubt may show.
When this occurs,
then fear and doubt must go.

To this I tell,
resist fear and doubt.
Come against them in the name of Jesus,
and drive them out.

Keep your faith shield up.
Don't let it down.
For if you do,
it will cause you to frown.

Keep your faith switch turned on,
and maintain your peace.
Keep your faith switch turned on,
and through your mouth release.

It's not always easy,
but when you do,
it pleases God,
and He'll reward you.

DECEMBER 11

MESSAGE FROM ADAM

I recall the story of Adam.
He took the apple from Eve.
This was shortly after,
Eve had been deceived.

God had told them both,
don't eat of that tree.
God's message was clear,
it was easy to perceive.

So Adam knew the truth.
He didn't have to eat of the fruit.
He could have said no,
and not followed suit.

It's the woman you gave me, God.
It's her fault.
That's how he reacted,
when they got caught.

Adam did like many today.
He tried to shift blame,
in a quick effort,
to hide his shame.

Throughout societies today,
people won't accept responsibility,
for their actions and deeds.
In these cases, they lack maturity.

A man will never mature,
if he is not able to accept responsibility,
for his actions and deeds.
It comes with maturity.

Adam has a message for society.
For your actions be responsible.
Don't shift blame,
when you stand accountable.

DECEMBER 12

PROTECT YOUR POSSESSION

Look at an armored car,
when it comes to a bank.
It's well protected,
like a small tank.

The guards are armed,
with weapons at waist.
They get out quickly,
with much haste.

Get the money in,
and secured in place.
They work efficiently,
at a quick pace.

This cargo is considered important.
Thus man protects it well.
This provides a good point,
for us to dwell.

Things of value,
man will protect.
Assault on valued possessions,
he will reject.

The Word can be compared,
to nuggets of gold,
when you get it down in your spirit,
and in your soul.

To this I ask,
should not the Word be protected?
Attempts at theft,
must always be rejected.

You've worked too hard.
You've gained much from your Bible studying.
You've gained much by listening and hearing,
under good teaching.

To this I say,
value the Word.
Value the promises and truth,
of what you've read and heard.

Guard your eyes, ears and mouth.
Protect you possession.
Don't give the devil,
any kind of concession.

DECEMBER 13

THE GREATEST DISCOVERY

Explorers set sail,
across oceans of deep.
Tough weather was faced,
both cold and heat.

Great effort was made,
as they endured,
the wrath of storms,
and discoveries secured.

Inventors worked hard,
throughout all time,
looking for discoveries,
to benefit mankind.

Trying to help man,
scientists gave their lives,
seeking medical discoveries,
to help man survive.

Many miners worked hard,
as it has been told,
prospecting the hills,
trying to discover gold.

The pursuit of oil,
was seen on the plains,
where man worked hard,
in a similar vein.

When discoveries were made,
there was great jubilation,
but they don't compare,
to that of salvation.

The greatest discovery,
on this man's earth,
is that Jesus died for him,
to provide him the new birth.

This discovery is priceless,
and yet is free.
This discovery is available,
for you and me.

If you haven't already,
then receive God's love.
It's earth's greatest discovery,
that was sent from above.

DECEMBER 14

WORRY

All care and concern is not sinful.
Concern that causes attendance to business,
is the responsible way.
Concern that causes worry, anxiety and fear,
is the unbiblical way.

Worry must be recognized as sinful,
it is unnecessary.
It has roots of unbelief,
for God is able and trustworthy.

Worry is forbidden by God,
and can cause sickness.
It is a thief of time,
as its focus will witness.

Worry is unbecoming for a believer,
it focuses on earthly values, not eternal.
Excessively attacking tomorrow's problems
assumes responsibility,
and will wastefully drive energy through life's
funnel.

It must be remembered,
that God is a Christian's provider.
It's important to focus on the bounty of God,
if you're a believer.

Remind yourself of God's provision,
and control your thought life.
Develop a thankful and praising spirit,
and remember you're in Christ.

Redirect your energies,
and pray and trust.
Be confident in God's Word,
for it's a must.

Plan for tomorrow,
and trust God to direct.
Trust in His provision,
and you'll be set.

DECEMBER 15

I DON'T WANT AN UMBRELLA

Don't give me an umbrella,
to shield me from this rain.
If I wanted a shield,
then I would not gain.

This rain isn't wet.
I can't feel it by touch,
but it's a wonderful rain,
that I appreciate so much.

Fill me with this rain,
it is my plea.
To receive this rain,
brings me great glee.

From clouds it won't come,
of this I know,
but I know of its source,
if to the Bible I go.

It's the rain of the Holy Spirit,
of which I speak.
It's a rain that I encourage,
for all to seek.

Of this I can tell you,
you won't be the same,
if you'll open your heart,
and receive this rain.

It's offered to you,
and is available to all,
but you must come to the Lord,
and on Him do call.

So come to the Lord,
and with speed do go.
It's a rain you should want,
so don't be slow.

DECEMBER 16

LEAVE YOUR PALACE

Nehemiah asked the king,
if he could rebuild the walls,
of the city of Jerusalem,
like before its fall.

The condition of Jerusalem,
was of one of destruction,
so the king granted favor,
and offered no obstruction.

Nehemiah left the comforts,
of his palace home,
and along with others,
he was soon gone.

They were determined to succeed,
and were unified in mind,
as they rebuilt the walls,
that had been ravaged through time.

The walls of society,
are like Jerusalem's walls.
They've been torn down,
and have suffered great fall.

The condition isn't good,
and it's easy to see,
that great oppression is working,
against humanity.

Laborers are needed,
to unify in mind,
and rebuild the walls,
that have been ravaged through time.

Laborers with zeal,
and commitment to intercede,
are needed for society,
for plans to succeed.

Souls are hurting,
but Christians can effect change,
in a hurting society,
that is experiencing much pain.

DECEMBER 17

REMEMBER HIS TITLE

Material things of the world,
certainly qualify,
to serve as idols,
as people try to satisfy.

Looking for human idols,
Hollywood is one source,
and don't forget about sports,
but of course.

Don't forget about activities.
Some may cause obsession.
When this occurs,
they'll take time possession.

Do you have idols?
I'm not talking golden calf.
Let's examine your way of living,
and walk down this path.

Take a look at your time,
and how it's spent.
Isolating your time,
will show how you're bent.

Check the desires,
down in your heart.
Is there room for Jesus?
Let's check each part.

If there's anything over Jesus,
that takes priority,
then you better examine it,
and make it more of a minority.

Don't replace Christ,
with some idol.
Make Him Lord,
and remember His title.

DECEMBER 18

IS THERE NOT A CAUSE?

David approached the Israelites,
that were gathered in battle array,
and when he heard Goliath's taunts,
he had much to say.

Is there not a cause,
to take a stand,
against this Philistine,
who is a heathen man?

He has no covenant with God,
and curses God's Name.
Why does the army of the Lord,
stand here in shame?

God is with us,
and sees his taunts.
Why does Israel condone,
these audacious flaunts?

David went forth,
and conquered his foe,
even though the others,
refused to go.

Is there not a cause,
in our era of life,
to take a bold stand,
for our Lord Jesus Christ?

Is there not a cause,
to get on fire,
and do His work,
with Godly desire?

Is there not a cause,
to serve Him well,
so that others,
may be saved from Hell?

DECEMBER 19

I KNOW WHO YOU ARE

Let's go back in time,
and observe some scenes.
As you observe Jesus,
you will pick up some things.

Day after day,
Jesus went about doing good.
He tried to help others,
wherever He could.

He healed many,
and cast out demonic spirits.
He was the Son of God,
and the spirits knew it.

I think it interesting,
that before Jesus went to the cross,
that the demonic spirits knew Him,
before He died for the lost.

"You are the Son of God,"
you would have heard,
from the voices of demons,
or some similar words.

Even before the cross,
the demonic spirits knew.
They recognized Him,
without any clues.

They knew that Jesus,
was no ordinary man.
They would later watch Jesus,
reveal God's masterful plan.

The demons know,
that Jesus died on the cross for you.
The demons know it,
but do you?

Jesus has spoken to your heart,
on more than one occasion.
Don't ignore His tugs,
or reply with derision.

Receive Him as Lord,
and accept His invitation,
to receive eternal life,
and His plan of salvation.

DECEMBER 20

SEEK TO EXCEL

Watch a master craftsman,
busy with tools.
Some things will be seen,
that aren't learned in schools.

Notice his eyes,
and preciseness of hands.
Top quality is sought,
by a master craftsman.

The wood is smoothed,
with a touch of perfection.
He confronts mediocrity,
with immediate rejection.

There's a certain spirit,
that seems to pervade,
whether work is done,
in sun or shade.

It's a spirit of excellence,
of which I refer.
You're typically find it,
when you see excellence occur.

Mediocrity is fine,
if you're just trying to get by,
but Christians are called,
to greater standards of high.

Christians take heed,
as you hear these words.
Ponder awhile,
on what you just heard.

Wherever you're placed,
or wherever you dwell,
put forth the effort,
to always excel.

DECEMBER 21

RUSTLER OR SHEEP THIEF

Rustling was harshly treated,
back in western days.
In the eyes of the law,
it was a criminal way.

Taking a man's livestock,
was not overlooked.
It wasn't a good deed,
no matter how many took.

When I consider some pastors,
I think of this.
I've some points to make,
that should not be missed.

Stealing sheep,
is not pleasing to Christ.
Better evaluate this,
or it could affect your life.

Don't raid another man's flock.
Taking sheep of similar belief,
is not walking in love,
it makes you a thief.

Don't fool yourself.
This is a misdeed.
You answer to Christ,
for the way you lead.

Let Christ build His church.
The pastor is a servant.
Feed the flock he has given you,
and don't be irreverent.

Walk in love.
Christ will send people your way.
Don't raid another man's flock.
This is important to say.

DECEMBER 22

CARES OF THE WORLD

Cares of the world,
can have a robbing affect,
on the things of God,
with negative effect.

People of God,
are not to be hindered,
by the cares of the world,
and what they render.

Cast those cares,
on the shoulders of God.
He's waiting for them,
so to you I'll prod.

He'll handle each one,
as His Word does say.
Cast them now,
cast them today.

No need to worry,
God now has those cares.
Rest in peace,
and don't be scared.

Receive God's Word,
revealed as truth.
Deep into your heart,
let it take root.

Move with confidence,
and remain carefree.
If you really think about it,
it's the way you should be.

No need to get shook,
God is at work on your behalf.
He's taking care of those cares,
that to Him you cast.

DECEMBER 23

I HAVE A QUESTION

I have a question,
where did the wind go?
It was here,
just an hour ago.

I have a question,
where did the rain go?
It was here,
just an hour ago.

I have a question,
where did the birds go?
They were here,
just a week ago.

I have a question,
where did the leaves go?
They were on the trees,
just a month ago.

Life is filled with questions,
and patterns of change.
It will always be so,
for life in this plane.

It continues to the end,
even when life makes its final change.
For you see in death,
questions still pertain.

I have a question,
where did John go?
He was alive,
just a day ago?

I have a question,
I would like to know,
when you die,
where will you go?

DECEMBER 24

THOUGHTS FOR SELF-IMPROVEMENT

Do not be harsh or judgmental against people,
in negative attitude or speech.
Make no false misleading or deceptive statements,
for this is not the path to seek.

Control impatience or anger towards others,
while seeking constructive solutions.
Don't allow any spirit of bitterness or slander take root,
but kick it out with complete eviction.

Be subject to one another,
in your mind and spirit.
Always be a source of encouragement,
and biblical comfort.

Be able to forgive,
and never hold a grudge.
Maintain spiritual insight,
and from malice totally budge.

Help others overcome,
and be a good brother in Christ.
Lift up their burdens,
and don't ignore their cries.

Develop a spirit of excellence,
for it is Christ's way.
Your work and actions,
always have much to say.

Share the gospel,
and support the Lord's work.
You're part of His team,
so do your part in His work.

Remain strong in the Lord,
through use of daily and quality time.
Always remember time spent with Him,
is never wasted time.

DECEMBER 25

OVER THE EDGE

I remember a visit,
I once made to Niagara Falls.
I will now tell you,
in my mind what I saw.

I looked up Niagara River,
and I saw peoples' heads,
flowing down the river,
the way it was led.

Their faces had smiles,
with no apprehension of danger.
It looked like they were enjoying themselves,
with no tension of linger.

The current was strong,
and flowed swiftly by.
As the people approached the edge,
there weren't any sighs.

It's when they went over the edge,
that I noticed a change.
Their faces were now much different,
and didn't look the same.

As they tumbled over,
their faces filled with fear,
and the meaning of these thoughts,
then became crystal clear.

Death had seized their lives,
and now peril had set in,
all because,
they weren't redeemed from sin.

These people freely lived their lives,
without the acceptance of Jesus Christ.
They're now doomed forever,
in the afterlife.

DECEMBER 26

INTENSELY INVOLVED

What would you call one,
who monitored all of your actions?
Surely you would be impressed,
with this kind of attention.

What would you call one,
who wants you to always do well?
Surely you would appreciate it,
and think it swell.

What would you call one,
who is on duty towards you 24 hours a day?
Surely you would have some comments,
with some nice words to say.

What would you call one,
who consistently works towards your good?
Most people would like this,
as certainly they should.

What would you call one,
who hurts when you hurt?
A cry from you,
reaches this one with touch.

What would you call one,
who has such a great amount of love,
for you and your well-being,
as only could come from above?

What would you call one,
who died on the cross,
so that you could be saved,
and not be eternally lost?

Take no more time to ponder,
and attempt to solve.
You call him Jesus,
who towards you is intensely involved.

DECEMBER 27

PRESCRIPTION FOR SUCCESS

A prescription for success,
is found in the Bible.
It's found in the Book of Joshua,
and will ensure survival.

Keep the Word before you,
ever in your sight.
Meditate on it,
both day and night.

From your mouth,
do not let it depart,
for as you speak,
it gets down in your heart.

Be a doer of the Word,
and have great success,
for it will protect you,
and keep you out of a mess.

A prosperous future is yours,
if these words you heed.
You'll find the Father,
will meet all your needs.

Keep track of your time,
and how it is used.
Don't allow your time,
to become wasted or abused.

If you're too busy,
to have time for the Lord,
then I recommend you consider,
the words you've just heard.

Evaluate your schedule.
Determine what must go,
and your quality decision,
will begin to show.

Know for sure,
it's time well spent,
as blessings begin to show,
from Heaven sent.

Set time aside,
again I say,
and you'll have great success,
if you do it God's way.

DECEMBER 28

RIGHT FRIENDSHIPS ARE IMPORTANT

People have an affect,
and will reinforce,
values that come,
from their inner source.

That's why it's important,
not to be misled,
and run with the wrong company,
in light of words said.

Iron sharpens iron,
in a positive sense,
but the same can be said,
in the negative sense.

Wrong friendships,
even with negative Christians,
will have an affect,
if they can get you to listen.

A little bit here,
and a little bit there,
will begin to add up,
without much flare.

Wrong thinking will creep in,
and it'll dampen your walk,
and soon you'll notice,
it'll affect your talk.

A diligent and strong Christian,
should seek comparable friends.
He'll be helped and encouraged,
with the messages they send.

Right friendships are important,
and will affect your course.
It'll serve you well,
to have faith reinforced.

DECEMBER 29

ON YOUR KNEES

Look at the newspapers,
and you'll see real gloom.
Look at the television,
and you'll see real doom.

Problems and more problems,
will show their heads.
Many people question,
how this country is led.

Solutions are sought,
but consistently fall short,
as the leaders analyze,
but with negative report.

Christians know the answer,
that professional politicians lack.
Step number one, it's unto God,
that this nation must come back.

One of the most important things,
that Christians can do,
is to consistently pray for this nation,
and with commitment remain true.

Prayer is essential,
and will effect change,
if God's people,
will pray in His Name.

Christians need to unify,
and pray with fervency.
Christians need to pray,
for there is urgency.

Lift up this nation,
and lift it up now.
God can effect change,
for He knows how.

Don't become lax,
or even nonchalant,
believing others will do it,
for many will not.

Receive these words,
and make it a point,
to begin praying for this nation,
if change you want.

DECEMBER 30

TRAILBLAZER

No path was there,
so as a trailblazer he came,
to redeem man,
and save him from shame.

Great sacrifice was required,
on His personal part,
so He could change,
the state of men's hearts.

Based on the God's plan,
He would leave His home,
and proceed to earth,
for a short season to roam.

With purpose He came,
to clear the path,
between God and man,
that will eternally last.

Obstacles were there,
but the path was cleared.
You might say,
He was the ultimate pioneer.

Much cost was involved,
to blaze this trail,
but it was required,
since Adam fell.

All this was done,
as a result of love,
that's why He came,
from His home above.

Yes, Jesus went ahead,
and paved the way,
so that mankind,
could be saved.

DECEMBER 31

DREAM BIG

Take a look into your heart,
and check your desires.
Look for something,
that has some fire.

Now take that desire,
and begin to dream.
Within your mind,
make it seen.

Begin to envision,
that dream as real.
Desires fulfilled,
bring great thrill.

The desires of your heart,
are important to you.
You know this statement,
is certainly true.

They're also important to God,
for He loves you so.
He wants them fulfilled,
and will help them grow.

Hook up with God,
and take this to heart.
Dream real big,
and let God do His part.

You have a big God,
Who says all things are possible.
Accept this as fact,
and not merely plausible.

Dream real big.
Just let it go.
Hook up with God,
and dreams will show.

CONCLUSION

I realize this was a devotional; however in conclusion, I think it still extremely important to reference the most important decision in one's life. If there is any doubt as to your salvation, then I urge you to consider the following scriptures.

"As it is written, There is none righteous, no, not one." (Romans 3:10). "For all have sinned, and come short of the glory of God." (Romans 3:23).

"For the wages of sin is death; but the gift of God is eternal life through Jesus Christ our Lord." (Romans 6:23).

"For there is one God, and one mediator between God and men, the man Christ Jesus." (I Timothy 2:5).

"That if thou shalt confess with thy mouth the Lord Jesus, and shalt believe in thine heart that God hath raised him from the dead, thou shalt be saved. For with the heart man believeth unto righteousness; and with the mouth confession is made unto salvation." (Romans 10:9–10).

Now, here's a Sinner's Prayer to receive Jesus as Lord and Savior. Please repeat the following prayer and mean it from your heart. You must then be sincere, or they will only be words and mean nothing. If you are sincere, then God is sincere because God always honors His Word.

"Dear Heavenly Father, I come to You in the name of the Lord Jesus Christ. I ask You to forgive me of all my sins. I accept Jesus as my Lord and Savior and believe in my heart that He died on the cross for my sins and that You raised Him from the dead so that I could have right standing with You. I now repent and confess Jesus as my Lord and Savior. I thank You for giving me eternal salvation and ask that You would help me in my Christian walk."

I strongly encourage you to read your Bible daily to get to know the Lord better, talk to God daily in prayer, and find a church where the Bible is taught as the complete Word of God. I also encourage you to be water baptized.

About the Author

Commander Michael H. Imhof, U.S. Navy (ret.), was born in Fort Bragg, North Carolina and raised in Blasdell, New York. He attended the State University College of New York at Buffalo, where he received a Bachelor of Science degree. He was commissioned in 1973. After completing Basic Underwater Demolition/SEAL training in Coronado, California, Commander Imhof was assigned to SEAL Team TWO, and subsequent Naval Special Warfare and other type commands.

Commander Imhof, possessing a Naval Special Warfare designator, has served throughout the world in numerous positions. Assignments include Platoon Commander, Training Officer, Operations Officer, Staff Officer, Executive Officer and Commanding Officer. He also earned a Master's Degree in Administration from George Washington University and served as an instructor at the U.S. Naval Academy. His awards include Defense Meritorious Service Medal; Meritorious Service Medal with two Gold Stars in lieu of second and third awards; Joint Service Commendation Medal; Navy Commendation Medal with Gold Star in lieu of second award; United Nations Medal; and other service awards.

A military officer of strong Christian convictions, Commander Imhof is ready and willing to share his faith with all. He is convinced that the Bible is the authoritative and uncompromising Word of God and gives thanks for the wonderful blessings of God in his life and the lives of his family. He is an active member in his local church.

Other books include *Lessons from Bible Characters, More Lessons from Bible Characters, Supernatural Testimonies, Testimonies of Ex-Muslims, Stand Up for God, God's Word: Bulletproof*, and *Pushing Against Darkness*.

We invite you to view the complete selection of titles we publish at:
www.ASPECTBooks.com

We encourage you to write us with your thoughts about this, or any other book we publish at:
info@ASPECTBooks.com

ASPECT Books' titles may be purchased in bulk quantities for educational, fund-raising, business, or promotional use.
bulksales@ASPECTBooks.com

Finally, if you are interested in seeing your own book in print, please contact us at:
publishing@ASPECTBooks.com

We are happy to review your manuscript at no charge.

www.ingramcontent.com/pod-product-compliance
Lightning Source LLC
LaVergne TN
LVHW061244100826
845148LV00008B/1024

* 9 7 8 1 5 7 2 5 8 2 2 2 4 *